Praying by the Book

Reading the Psalms

Praying by the Book

Reading the Psalms

Edited by

Craig Bartholomew

and

Andrew West

paternoster
press

Paternoster Press is an imprint of Paternoster Publishing,
P.O. Box 300, Carlisle, Cumbria, CA3 0QS, UK
and
P.O. Box 1047, Waynesboro, GA 30830–2047, USA
Website: www.paternoster-publishing.com

British Library Cataloguing in Publication Data
A catalogue record for this book is available from the British Library

ISBN 1–84227–129–6

Cover Design by Gert Swart and Zak Benjamin, South Africa
Typeset by WestKey Ltd, Falmouth, Cornwall
Printed in Great Britain by Bell & Bain, Glasgow

Contents

Foreword

It is my great pleasure to write a foreword to this volume. The Psalms have a special place in the life and worship of the Church and, over the centuries, Christians have found in this treasury reflections on the human condition which have challenged and comforted, shocked and sustained.

This volume originates in a Lenten course in the village of Oakridge in the Cotswolds where a large number of local people came together to study and seek to understand what meaning the Psalms have for Christians today. I commend the Revd Dr Craig Bartholomew, Research Fellow at the University of Gloucestershire, and the Revd Andrew West, University Chaplain, for their initial and continuing interest in the project.

All the contributors are staff or research students at the University; all of them are seeking to explore the enduring truths of the Psalms with the tools and insights of recent scholarship; all begin from the premise that the form of the Psalter itself, in addition to its component parts, has insights to offer about God's relationship with his people. As a worshipper who has experienced many such series over the years, I have found that this approach has at various levels challenged my understanding of the place of the Book of Psalms within the Biblical Canon.

The intention throughout is to make scholarship within the academy accessible to the inquiring reader who wishes to explore key aspects of the journey of faith. It will be an exciting and demanding journey with planned opportunities for guided reflection at each milestone. At the journey's end there will also be fresh insights into the influence of the Psalms within the Christian tradition over the centuries and within lives of individuals, whatever their tradition or context.

Dame Janet Trotter
Principal of the University of Gloucestershire

Preface

The Bible is an amazing book. In it we not only hear God addressing us, but we are also told how to respond to God amidst the ups and downs of our lives. The book of Psalms, in particular, is a library of resources for life with God. God's people have always found the Psalms a place that they keep returning to in order to find God once again amidst the challenges of life. This book aims to make some of the best recent work on the Psalms available to Christians in order to deepen and strengthen their use of the psalms.

Academic study of the Bible and the devotional use of the Bible in the church do not always fit well together. Often they are deeply suspicious of each other. All the contributors to *Praying By the Book: Reading the Psalms* lament the bad relationship that sometimes exists between biblical studies and the use of the Bible in the church. There is a lot of biblical study nowadays that is not very helpful. However, there is also work being done that is quite outstanding. A good example of this is the work done on the book of the Psalms in the last twenty years or so. In the last few decades a growing number of scholars have done some brilliant work on reading the book of Psalms as a whole.

To many of us it might seem strange to think of the book of Psalms as a book, with a beginning, a middle and an ending. However, there is growing evidence that the book of Psalms is more than a collection of individual Psalms; rather it is a carefully arranged whole. And, most significantly, our reading of the individual Psalms is greatly enriched by taking note of the shape of the whole.

In *Praying By the Book* we seek to make some of these exciting new developments accessible at a church level. The chapters that make up this book were originally given as a Lenten series arranged by the church in Oakridge in the Cotswolds. Each week at Oakridge Methodist hall on a dark, Lenten evening some fifty of us would gather to look again at the Psalms. It has been heartening to see the hunger for the Word in our local churches.

Using this book

In order to make this book useful for churches, groups and the individual, we have divided each chapter up into five sections with a few questions for reflection after each section. In order to be nourished by the Psalms they need to be prayed and chewed over! Our hope is that even for the individual reader, these sections will encourage him or her to stop and reflect at these points.

If this book is being used in a group our suggestion is that each group member reads a section a day for five days of the week, that the group meets on another day and uses the group questions at the end to guide their discussions – the remaining day of the week being Sunday! Each group will need to adjust their use of this book for their own context. In our Lenten course we started with coffee and tea, followed by the study and then a carefully prepared 15 minutes or so of worship response to the study. It is always important to give time to use our reflections upon the Psalms to respond to God, even if that simply means ten minutes or so of quiet reflection before God.

The Pictures

Art can be very helpful in our reflections upon Scripture. A distinguished South African sculptor, Gert Swart and his wife Istine, worked closely with us in developing this book. Gert drew the pictures you will find with each chapter and designed the cover which was painted by South African artist Zak Benjamin. We have written a few lines with each picture as an aid to understanding them. We encourage readers to use the pictures to help them reflect upon the meaning of the Psalms for their lives. We fully recognise that some will find this more helpful then others – this is as it should be. The important thing is that we engage with Scripture as God's Word.

Thanks

Many people have helped in the production of this book. To Mr Alan Dyer, Rev Ian Farrow, the church in Oakridge and the other local churches involved in the Lenten talks – many thanks. Without your invitation to do these talks and support of them this book would never have seen the light of day. Rev Judy Howard made a wonderful contribution in the worship responses she organised for each talk. We are also most grateful to the artists (Gert and Zak) and to the speakers/authors who have been so co-operative in the work involved in finalising the text of this book. Helen Henderson and Rosemary Hales helped us make the text as accessible as possible. As always, Tony Graham of Paternoster has been a pleasure to work with. Finally, we are most grateful to Dame Janet Trotter, Principal of the University of Gloucestershire, where all the authors work, for her support and for her willingness to write the foreword to this book. Our hope and prayer is that this small offering will redirect us to the Psalms as food and drink for the journey of our lives.

Andrew West and Craig Bartholomew

Contributors

Craig Bartholomew is research fellow in the School of Theology and Religious Studies at the University of Gloucestershire. He is also an Anglican minister, associated with All Saints Parish Church in Bisley, near Stroud. Craig specializes in biblical interpretation and in understanding our culture today.

Zak Benjamin is a painter and printmaker. His work is both humorous and profoundly relevant. He employs a unique palette of wondrous colours. He lives in Gauteng, South Africa.
http://www.zakbenjaminartist.homestead.com/index.html

Jamie Grant, a Scotsman, is working towards a PhD in Old Testament (focusing on the Psalms) at the University of Gloucestershire. He and wife Iwona met in Poland, where they both worked for the IFES student movement, and they have two young daughters and an even younger son. He enjoys sports of all kinds (mostly watching, some participating), reading, coffee, cinema and playing with his kids … not necessarily in that order!

Gert Swart was born in Durban, South Africa, where he qualified and worked as a public health inspector before studying fine art for two years at the Natal Technikon. He now resides and works as a sculptor in Pietermaritzburg, RSA. He is married to Istine Rodseth.

Gordon McConville has taught the Old Testament at Trinity College, Bristol and Wycliffe Hall, Oxford, and now at the University of Gloucestershire. His main scholarly interest is in Deuteronomy, but he has written on a number of Old Testament books for a general readership, including two volumes in the Daily Study Bible series (*Chronicles* and *Ezra, Nehemiah, Esther*).

Karl Möller comes from northern Germany. He moved to England in 1994 to do a doctorate in Old Testament studies. He is a researcher in the School of Theology and Religious Studies at the University of Gloucester-shire. Karl has written on the prophets and on literary hermeneutics and he enjoys good literature. Married with two children, he is always on the hunt for the latest cookbook.

Gordon Wenham is Professor of Old Testament at the University of Gloucestershire and has written commentaries on *Genesis, Leviticus* and *Numbers.* He is the author of *Story as Torah* and has co-authored *Jesus and Divorce.* Married with four children, he is also a Lay Reader in the Church of England and enjoys gardening.

Andrew West is Chaplain of the University of Gloucester-shire. Prior to his present appointment he was in parochial ministry in Church of England parishes in Lancashire and Warwickshire. Many years ago he used to teach Economics. He enjoys reading, fell walking, travelling and cooking and recently enjoyed his first attempt at hang-gliding.

The Cover

Rich Old Testament and Jewish imagery is used to alert us to the potential of the Psalms – symbolised by the scroll in the left hand corner – in our lives. The broken wall, perhaps evoking the destruction of Jerusalem when Israel was taken into exile in the Old Testament (Neh. 1:3), reminds us that life can be tough and mysterious. Life is broken, not least because of our sinfulness. But our God is a God of reconstruction and salvation: note the horns (of salvation, Ps. 18:2) at the top of the cover, and the candelabra (symbolizes God's presence, Exodus 37:17–24) like tree (Ps. 1:3) growing out of the wall, and the rainbow (Gen. 9:12–17) through the title. The circle created by 'Praying By the Book' indicates the wholeness that God's salvation brings to our lives and societies. However, for this wholeness to materialize we need the Psalms to be active in our lives: the scroll of the Psalms is encased and needs to be opened!

Introduction

Craig Bartholomew

Today, as has been the case down the centuries, Christians continue to find in the psalms a vocabulary for responding to God amidst the seasons and challenges of life. Eugene Peterson rightly says that 'The great and sprawling university that Hebrews and Christians have attended to learn to answer God, to learn to pray, has been the Psalms.'[1] One only has to reflect on a psalm like Psalm 23 to see how indebted we are to the psalms in our lives with God. As Esther de Waal says:

> In the psalms I find myself at my worst and my best. Here I can acclaim God with warmth and confidence and hope, but here also I can give vent to those black thoughts that might otherwise lie hidden in the dark and angry corners of my heart. Above all the psalms express the reality of my longing for God and my joy and sufferings in the vicissitudes of my search for him. Sometimes God is close, sometimes distant. I seek him in the desert and on the mountain, in poverty and in emptiness and in waiting. Today God is mindful of me, tomorrow he may not visit me. Today I am brought to the mountain top, tomorrow I am calling from

the depths. Today I am radiant, tomorrow I face darkness. Today I enjoy life, tomorrow I feel the hand of death.[2]

In many of the books of the Bible we hear God's call to be his people and to live as his people. However, in the psalms we are instructed how to *answer* that call amidst all the challenges of life. The great Catholic theologian Hans Urs von Balthasar articulates this aspect of the Bible very clearly in his book *On Prayer*:

> Prayer is a dialogue, not a monologue recited by men in God's presence … What do we do, when at prayer, but speak to a God who long ago revealed himself to man in a word so powerful and all-embracing that it can never be solely of the past, but continues to resound through the ages? The better we learn to pray, the more we are convinced that our halting utterance to God is but an answer to God's speech to us; and so *it is only in God's language that we can commune with him*. … Just consider a moment: is not the "Our Father", by which we address him each day, his own word? Was it not given us by the Son of God, himself God and the Word of God? Could any man by himself have discovered such language? … What could we possibly have said to God, if he had not already communicated and revealed himself to us in his word, giving us access to and commerce with him? … Prayer, we can now see, is communication, in which God's word has the initiative and we, at first, are simply listeners. Consequently, what we have to do is, first, listen to God' word and then, through that word, learn how to answer.[3]

Like the Lord's Payer, the Psalms are God's word to us telling us how to respond to his word to us! In his journals at a certain point, Thomas Merton notes how perfectly Psalm 54:4–9 expresses his feelings:

> 'There is nothing I have ever written or could write that expresses so completely the depths of the own soul than these verses ... All five lines are truer of my life than anything I have ever written, and this gives me great confidence in the liturgy. This is the secret of the Psalms. Our identity is hidden in them. In them we find ourselves and God. In these fragments he has revealed not only Himself to us but ourselves to Him.'[4]

Similarly when Merton is feeling penitent, he notes that 'The psalms say this better than I ever could. I am sorry that it has taken me so long to begin to discover the psalms. I am sorry that I have not lived in them. Their words are full of the living waters of those true tears with which You taught the Samaritan your mercy.'[5] The Psalter is a marvellous handbook for the journey, instructing us how to maintain perspective and how to retain a dynamic relationship with God through the valleys and the peaks of life. The psalms induct us into the practice of the presence of God and life-long prayer.

However, we do tend to read the psalms as individual prayers or songs, and we hardly ever take note of the fact that each one is part of the larger book of Psalms and part of one of the five books into which the Psalter is divided! Christians are aware nowadays that it is always important to read Bible verses in their contexts, lest we misread them and they become a pretext for us getting our own way! However, when it comes to the psalms the rule about context gets ignored. Eugene Peterson rightly observes that we miss out on God's instruction when we fail to notice the context in which psalms occur:

> There is one large fact about the Psalms that requires notice before attending to the actual reading and praying of them – their arrangement. One hundred and fifty Psalms are arranged in five books. The arrangement is impossible to miss, but like many other obvious but familiar things, we commonly fail to notice it. But notice is what is required: the five-book arrangement establishes the conditions under which we will pray, shaping a canonical context for prayer ... The significance of the five-book arrangement cannot be overstressed. It is not a minor and incidental matter of editorial tinkering; it is a major matter of orientation so that prayer will be learned properly as human answering speech to the addressing speech of God, and not to be confused or misunderstood as initiating speech.[6]

A quick flip through the Psalter in your Bible will reveal that they are indeed divided into five smaller books, made up of the following Psalms:

Book 1   Psalms 1–41
Book 2   Psalms 42–72
Book 3   Psalms 73–89
Book 4   Psalms 90–106
Book 5   Psalms 107–150

Each of the first four books ends with a liturgical formula with the elements 'Blessed be the LORD ... Amen.' At the end of Book 4 (see Psalm 106:48), the word hallelujah ('Praise the Lord') is added to this formula and praise becomes the consuming focus of Book 5. Eugene Peterson says of this move from 'Amen' (at the end of Books 1–4) to 'Hallelujah' (Book 5, see particularly Psalms 146–150):

> The shift from Amen to Hallelujah modulates the great Amen-affirmations of the first four books into a celebrative conclusion to the five-book Psalter. This grand conclusion bursts the confines of the liturgical formula and booms out five hallelujah Psalms (146–150), one for each 'book' of the Psalter. Each of these five concluding Psalms begins and ends with the Hallelujah. ... The last Psalm, the 150th, not only begins and ends but pivots each sentence on the Hallelujah: praise the Lord, praise God, praise him ... thirteen times – a cannonade of hallelujahs, booming salvos of joy.[7]

All this means that considerable effort went into the editing of the Psalter into its present shape. Each individual psalm would of course have had its own history. David may well, for example, have written Psalm 23 out of his experience as a shepherd, which he used to describe his walk with God. However, later editors have deliberately and thoughtfully arranged the psalms into the shape in which we now have them.

> All that editorial activity is evidence that prayer was getting a lot of attention in Israel. Providing the means by which people were taught and trained in prayer, responding to their God out of the specific actualities of their lives was high on the agenda, sharing top billing with the means for hearing the word itself.[8]

Thus, if we really want to benefit from the Psalter's teaching, we must attend to each psalm individually *and* also pay careful attention to the shape of the Psalter as a whole. Again, as Peterson says: 'The care and art that were taken to fashion the five-fold shape of the Psalter invites a great deal more hermeneutical attention than is usually given to it.'[9] But how precisely does focusing on the Psalter as a whole help us to understand the psalms?

First, the fact that there are five books in the Psalter may be very significant. The five-fold structure of the Psalter is probably modelled on the Pentateuch, the first *five* books of the Old Testament. In Hebrew the Pentateuch is called the *Torah* (instruction), indicating that it contains instruction from God – think of the stories about creation, the fall into sin, God's purposes with Abraham and all the laws in Exodus to Deuteronomy! The five-fold structure of the Psalter alerts us to the fact that to every word from God there must be an answering word from us. God's Word relates to all of our lives, individually and communally, and we are called to live out the totality of our lives before God.[10] Our lives are to be lived out as a response to God's word to us, and the psalms are there to instruct us in this response. 'Everything that a person can possibly feel, experience and say is brought into expression before God in the Psalms.'[11]

Secondly, we need to be aware that it is only recently that biblical scholars have really begun to explore the book of Psalms as a whole. When Eugene Peterson wrote *Working the Angles* (a book I have quoted from repeatedly in this introduction) back in 1987, he recognized the five-fold structure of the Psalter. But apart from this scheme, he thought the psalms were random and mixed. It is now clear, however, that in many cases the arrangement of the psalms is far from random. In the last fifteen years or so considerable work has been done, and continues to be done, on the shape of the Psalter as a whole, and a whole series of books, commentaries and article have appeared demonstrating how fruitful this line of research is for reading the psalms.

Much of this recent material is found in academic publications that the average church member will never read or want to read! In this book we aim to make some of the best recent work on the Psalms available at an accessible level for non-specialists. Thus, Craig Bartholomew explains the arguments for reading Psalms 1 and 2 as the introduction to the Psalter and shows how this leads us into the book as a whole. Gordon McConville takes us through Psalms 15–24 and demonstrates the rich rewards that follow from taking the context of the psalms seriously. Jamie Grant focuses on Psalms 73 and 89 and the theme of lament in the psalms. Gordon Wenham opens up for us the overarching theme of the reign of God in the Psalter, particularly as it comes into focus in Book 4. Andrew West leads us into the crescendo of praise that concludes the Psalter. Finally, Karl Möller looks at the way the psalms are used in the New Testament.

I should make a comment or two about *the style* of this book and how best to use it. Recent studies of the psalms have alerted us that they are *torah* (instruction). We generally think of the psalms as prayers and hymns, but the approach used in this book suggests that the Psalter is primarily instruction! The best way to understand this difference is, I think, to realize that prayer often rehearses, in relation to our circumstances, what we know about God before him.[12] You learn a lot about how people think about God and the world if you listen to the way they pray! This is the way in which the book of Psalms instructs us. As we read or listen to these prayers and hymns, we are instructed about the way the psalmists thought about God and the world and how they brought this to bear on their situations. Thus, the psalms are prayer *and* instruction!

The authors of this book are mainly academics, and we are generally good at analysing a book like the Psalms to see what precisely it has to teach us. That is, I think, the strength of the chapters that follow. They are strong on the psalms as instruction! However, it is absolutely crucial, if we are to be properly instructed by the psalms, that we turn their vision of God and the world back into prayer, and relate this vision to *our* situations. Thomas Merton describes this personal appropriation of the psalms as follows:

> We simply need to take possession of these Psalms, 'move in' to them, so to speak. Or rather we move them into the house of our own soul so that we think of our ordinary experiences in their light and with their own words.[13]

For this reason we have divided each chapter up into five sections, each section ends with some reflective questions and a prayer. There is also an activities suggestion at the end of each chapter. This is intended to help guide group and individual responses to the chapter as a whole. It would be a good idea to keep a notebook with you as you work through this book and reflect on the psalms. We suggest, especially for groups using this book, that group members read a section a day in preparation for the group meeting on the sixth day, the remaining day being Sunday!

We have also specially commissioned the cover for this book and a drawing to go with each chapter. Gert Swart and Zak Benjamin produced the cover, and Gert the drawings, from their reading of the psalms and the text of this book. Our hope is that the artwork will help stimulate your imagination, as you reflect on the psalms, and lead you back into God's presence.

A feast awaits in the Psalter! We hope that this book will help lead you into a deeper understanding of the psalms and a richer experience of and response to God.

Blessed be the LORD … Amen, Hallelujah!

REFLECTION

- Reflect on the way in which the Psalms have helped you in your journey with God up until now.
- Are there particular Psalms that you have returned to time and again? Make a list of them.
- Have you ever thought about the Psalter as a book with a beginning, a middle and an end? From the introduction do you think this could help you in your understanding of the psalms?

Use this verse from Psalm 119:18 to pray for understanding as you explore the Psalter:

> *Open my eyes, so that I may behold*
> *wondrous things out of your law.*

Notes

1. Eugene Peterson, *Working the Angles* (Grand Rapids: Eerdmans, 1987), 35.
2. Esther de Waal, *Seeking God: The Benedictine Way,* (London: Fount, 1984), 149.
3. (London: SPCK, 1961) 12. Italics mine.
4. Thomas Merton, *Entering the Silence: Becoming a Monk and Writer* (NY: HarperSanFrancisco, 1996) 383, 384.
5. Merton, Ibid., 420, 421.
6. Peterson, *Working,* 35.
7. Ibid., 36.
8. Ibid., 37.
9. Ibid.
10. Luther's delightful phrase for this is *coram deo* (before the face of God).
11. Peterson, *Working,* 39.
12. John Macquarrie rightly points out that prayer is a form of thinking. See his *Paths in Spirituality* (London: SCM, 1972), 25–39.
13. Thomas Merton, *Praying the Psalms* (Minnesota: Liturgical Press, 1956), 27.

The scroll (the book of the Psalms) has been opened for our instruction.
The waves remind us that life has many challenges. The tree (see Ps. 1:3,
Jer. 17:7,8) withstands the waves and flourishes.

PSALMS 1 AND 2 –
THE WAY OF BLESSING!

Craig Bartholomew

Psalms to read: Psalms 1,2,19,119

1. Blessed is ...

Psalm 1 begins with '*Blessed* is the person who' and Psalm 2 ends '*Blessed* are all who…'. We are familiar with statements beginning like this from the Sermon on the Mount; what we call 'the beatitudes' in Matthew 5:1–12. It has been suggested that 'Blessed is' should be understood as 'God approves' and this is helpful. These beatitudes describe a way of life of which God heartily approves and which therefore secures God's rich blessing. God, it could be said, has given us the Scriptures to tell us how to live a happy and successful life.[1] Such life is what the Psalms call 'blessed'.

If you are like me then you may feel a bit uneasy and sceptical at this point! The economies of our Western, consumerist societies depend on promoting products that offer the world, but never really deliver what they promise.[2] Too much contemporary Christianity has followed suit. Book after 'Christian' book offers Christianity as a quick fix to all our problems. By suggesting that the Psalms are about the way to blessing, are we not in danger of reading the Psalms in this way too? I hope not!

Psalms 1 and 2 *are* about blessedness. They are also the introduction to the Psalter as a whole, and this gives us an important clue about how the Bible defines blessing! In recent decades there has been a growing realization in biblical studies that however the biblical books came into existence they are now books in their own right. For example, David may have composed many of the Psalms while he worked as a shepherd or as king, but however they came into existence, they have now been edited into a book that we call the Psalms. We have already discussed this in the Introduction. In chapters that follow you will hear more about the case for reading the Psalter as a whole. Do note at this point that this approach does not deny the value of reading the Psalms as individual Psalms, but it does argue that taking note of where individual Psalms fit in to the Psalter as a whole greatly enriches our reading of the Psalms. An example of this is how to understand blessing.

Psalms 1 and 2 should be read together as the introduction to the Psalter as a whole. If this is so then the blessedness to which these psalms refer is not some simple product or experience that solves everything. The blessedness of Psalms 1 and 2, that will ultimately lead us to the symphony of praise that concludes the Psalter, pursues a route that takes us through the full range of human experience – through the psalms of lament, psalms that are desperate cries for help, psalms of depression and abandonment, and psalms of praise and joy. The whole gamut is there. If Psalms 1 and 2 call us to blessedness, it is clearly a blessedness that takes full account of the realities of life. That, in my opinion, is what makes this book so attractive. As Peterson says:

> I need a language that is large enough to maintain continuities and supple enough to express nuances across a lifetime that brackets child and adult experiences, and courageous enough to explore all the countries of sin and salvation, mercy and grace, creation and covenant, anxiety and trust, unbelief and faith that comprise the continental human condition. The Psalms are this large, supple, and courageous language. ... Everything that a person can possibly feel, experience, and say is brought into expression before God in the Psalms.[3]

REFLECTION

- The Psalms are about how to be blessed! What would be some wrong ways to understand 'blessed'? Make a list.
- Reflect on the picture at the start of this chapter.
  - In what ways would you like to be like the tree?
  - How do you feel about the waves in the picture?
  - Think of the waves in your life/ lives at present. How does God's blessing fit in with them?
  - How does the scroll in the picture (i.e. the book of Psalms) help with the waves?

A PRAYER:

> LORD, thank you that your way is the way of blessing.
> Thank you that you use all sorts of waves to secure our best interests.
> Help us to use the psalms to find your way in our lives.
> Amen.

2. *Instructed* by the LORD

What then, according to Psalm 1, is the way of blessedness?

The keyword in Psalm 1 is the Hebrew word torah (v.2). Most of our versions translate it as 'law.' It certainly includes God's commandments and laws but the meaning is the wider one of *instruction* in general. The point is that the blessed person develops a lifestyle which at root is instructed by Yahweh. The way of blessedness is a lifestyle, a way of instruction.

It is significant that God is here (Psalm 1:2) called LORD (Yahweh).[4] In the Old Testament LORD refers in particular to God as the one who rescued Israel from slavery in Egypt and established her in relationship to himself. As Exodus 19:4 puts it, the LORD carried the Israelites out of Egypt as an eagle carries its young on its back and brought her to himself! At Mount Sinai, God established Israel in a legal relationship with himself called a covenant, akin to a marriage relationship. God instructed Israel, through Moses, how the relationship would work so that they would know how to live a blessed existence, and Israel agreed to live in this way as God's people (see Exodus 20ff).

Thus, the blessed person is one who has been restored to a right relationship with God by his grace, and is now instructed by God as to how to live for God. For the Israelites, this instruction included all the laws and regulations they received with the covenants. For Christians today, God's instruction includes Jesus' teaching and all the other books of the New and Old Testaments. Being in covenant with God meant, for the Israelites, that God dwelt among them! This lent a freshness and a reality to God's instruction. Christians too should not think of the Bible as an impersonal code. The Spirit indwells the church and opens us up to the reality of God and makes the Scriptures come alive to us as God's living Word. However, it is important to be aware that it is primarily through the Scriptures that God continues to instruct us.

REFLECTION

- Think about all that God has done for you? What effect does this have upon you?
- Some people think that Christianity is first of all about rules. But firstly, it is about a relationship with God. Reflect on how God has 'brought you to himself', like he did with the Israelites.
- How does God's law (his instruction) fit in our relationship with God?

A PRAYER:

Thank you LORD
for bringing me to yourself.
Thank you that you are
My Father in heaven.
Teach me now to live as your child.
Amen.

3. Instructed by *the* LORD!!

When the Psalmist speaks of the blessed person as one who delights in the torah of Yahweh he *is* thinking of all the laws and instructions in the Old Testament. But lest we fear that this might be stifling, it is important to remember that Yahweh is also the creator God who made the world, and thus his instructions, always tie in with the shape he has given to the world. Scholars call Psalm 1 a wisdom psalm because of its emphasis on the torah of Yahweh. Psalms 19 and 119 are two other very significant wisdom Psalms which elaborate on the theme of torah/instruction.

Psalm 19 starts with creation (vv. 1–6) and then moves on to torah (vv. 7ff.). Scholars have often struggled with how vv. 7ff. relate to vv. 1–6. Clinton McCann gets it right, I think, when he says:

> When verses 7–13 are heard immediately following verses 1–6, the message about God's torah is clear. The 'instruction of the LORD' … is built into the very structure of the universe. It is as fundamental and reliable and close-at-hand as the progression of day and night (v.2), the rising and setting of the sun (v.6). And the impact of torah is just as far-reaching as the circuit of the sun – to the end of the heavens.[5]

McCann's proposed translation of Psalm 19:7 indicates the significance of this understanding: 'The instruction of the LORD is all-encompassing, restoring human life.'[6] To be instructed by Yahweh is not to become inhuman or a religious crank or a raving extrovert! God instructs us so that we might become the humans he always intended us to be. Hans Rookmaker, the late professor of art history at Amsterdam University, used to pose the question: Why does God save us? Why indeed? In terms of Psalm 1, we might ask: Why does God instruct us? Rookmaker's answer was simple: to make us fully human! And that too, if you like, is the answer of the Psalms. The Yahweh who would instruct us is the one of whose glory the heavens tell. And this instruction will help us to fit into the creation as he intended, to become fully human! McCann notes about Psalm 19:14, which is well known but hardly ever read in context, that 'this final verse is the psalmist's prayer that his or her life be in tune with the music of the spheres, the very structure of the universe'![7] That, no less, is the goal of Yahweh's instruction.

Not surprisingly, therefore, Yahweh's instruction is *all-pervasive* – it relates to life as a whole. We are so accustomed in the West to thinking of religion as a Sunday activity, a leisure thing which you do if it turns you on. But Yahweh's torah, cannot and will not be confined to one day a week. He is the author of life and his instruction relates to the whole of life. The all pervasiveness of torah comes out particularly in Psalm 119.

Note how Psalm 119 begins: Blessed are those whose way is blameless, who walk in the torah of Yahweh. Another beatitude! There are so many fascinating aspects of Psalm 119, and not least its structure, which is not evident in the English translations. The Psalm is made up of 22 stanzas, one for each letter of the Hebrew alphabet. In each stanza, each line begins with the same letter of the alphabet. Every stanza, except one (vv. 9–16), contains at least one occurrence of the word torah and every line of the Psalm contains either the word torah or a synonym. As McCann notes: 'The structure of Psalm 119 reinforces the theological content. In short, torah is pervasive and all-encompassing. It applies to everything from A to Z ...'[8] Yahweh's instruction is, thus, not only deeply human but also utterly comprehensive. Yahweh is the creator and he is sovereign over all of life. We will see below, when we come on to Psalm 2, that Yahweh's torah cannot be restricted to our private lives – it applies equally to politics and the life of the nations!

The way of blessedness, then, is a lifestyle rooted in and directed by the LORD, by the one who has rescued us from the slavery of sin and brought us to himself, in and through Jesus. Blessedness results from letting Yahweh's torah be our compass in all areas of life. Just what that involves, we will discuss further below and in later chapters. Certainly it should not be understood simplistically; and certainly it is not easy! – Check out Psalms like 73 and 88 and you will see what I mean. But already here in Psalm 1 the difficulty of a life of blessedness is apparent.

REFLECTION

- Do you find the idea of being instructed by the LORD exciting? How does the following saying from Irenaeus help to get you excited?

  The glory of God is the human person fully alive.

- In his useful book *On the Way: A Practical Theology of Christian Formation*, Les Steele says that 'Christian formation is real life. If we wall off our Christian formation from real life, we only pretend.'[9] Think how this section helps you to see that God's instruction cannot be separated off from real life.

A PRAYER (adapted from Numbers 6:24–26):

> LORD, *as I humble myself to be instructed by you,*
> *bless me and keep me,*
> *make your face to shine upon me,*
> *and be gracious to me,*
> *lift up your countenance upon me,*
> *and give me peace.*
> *Amen.*

4. *Choosing* blessing!

Psalm 1 starts in the first person (vv. 1–3), although some translations ignore this. 'Blessed is the person who ... his delight ... he meditates ... he is like a tree ... he prospers.' The lifestyle of this individual is contrasted immediately with that of the wicked – 'they' (plural) – in verse 4! Only in v. 6 are the righteous considered as a group and described in the plural as 'the righteous'.

Here in vv. 1–5 we have what is called *the doctrine of the two ways*; the way of the righteous (singular) and, by contrast, the way of the wicked (plural). Both are options, both give instruction (note 'advice' in v. 1) and both have established traditions ('the path that sinners tread', v. 1). The Psalmist is adamant, however, that the way of the wicked, of sinners, of scoffers is not the way to go – it is not fruitful now and (v. 6) under God's gaze it perishes. But, this side of eternity the way of the wicked remains an option! And that I think this is why Psalms 1 begins with the individual in focus. Let me explain.

Although being a Christian always involves being part of a community, it is as individuals that we have to decide that we will, by God's grace, follow the way of blessedness and not continue along the broad road that leads to destruction. Conversion is generally an individual affair, but once converted we discover that we are part of a community, the church. However, even when we are part of the church, it can be tempting to lapse back towards the broad path of the majority so that individual commitment remains important. That, I think, is why the Psalms begins by reminding us that the way of blessing involves each of us individually making the choice to go God's way. The Psalms is a handbook for those who have made this choice in life and who continue to make it from day to day.

Thus, some Psalms (e.g. Psalm 73, see chapter 3) explore the difficulties we experience in really seeing the dangers of the path of wickedness. The path of blessing is not always easy, but it is the way to go. It is a path characterised by instruction, by torah. The choice to go this way shows itself in a willingness to be instructed. Conversion involves coming to that point where we are willing to be taught by Yahweh, and the Christian path continues as it is begun – it is a life of discipleship, a life of being taught and growing in obedience. The one who delights in Yahweh's torah and meditates on it daily is blessed. The picture here is of a life grounded deeply in the living God. The wicked have no such foundation. McCann rightly says:

> Taking a clue from the central metaphor of Psalm 1, to be 'happy' or to 'prosper' is to have a solid foundation, to have a place to stand (vv. 1-5). For the Psalmist that foundation is to delight in and to meditate upon torah, to be constantly open to God's instruction. Taking such a stand or such a stance enables one to live with purpose and integrity in a world of confusion ... It enables one to live with hope in a world full of despair, and it enables one to perceive the mystery of life where others may perceive only the misery of life.[10]

REFLECTION

- Psalm 1 is about the choices we make to be instructed by the LORD rather than going our own way. Think about the choice you have made in your life/lives to follow God, and then reflect on that choice in the light of Peter's words to Jesus in John 6:68:

  Lord, to whom can we go? You have the words of eternal life.

- Use these verses from Psalm 119:10–11 to commit yourself again to your choice to follow God:

  > *With my whole heart I seek you*
  > *do not let me stray from your commandments.*
  > *I treasure your word in my heart,*
  > *So that I may not sin against you.*

5. Psalm 2 – Israel ... and the Nations

If Psalm 1 focuses primarily upon the way of blessedness for the individual believer, Psalm 2 is concerned with the people of Israel among the nations of the world. As Patrick Miller says:

> But now the ground has shifted and we do not hear about the individual who follows God's righteous way. Rather we hear the tumult of nations in league ... The world of kings and empires is in view, not the modes of personal and moral conduct.[11]

Scholars describe Psalm 2 as a royal psalm because it focuses on the Israelite king and his rule.[12] It has been suggested, rightly I think that this psalm was originally used during the coronation, or anointing, of a new king of Israel – it is stunning to imagine elements of Psalm 2 as part of a coronation liturgy (cf. vv. 7ff.). In Israel, the king and Yahweh were held closely together. The king had a special relationship with God. As Israel's leader, the king was the one who mediated Yahweh's rule over his people (cf. Deuteronomy. 17:14–20). Israel (God's people under God's rule) was, therefore, a symbol for God's plan for the whole creation (God's people living under God's reign in God's place).

Yahweh's rule did not, however, go down well among the nations (vv. 1–3.)! Indeed in Hebrew the word for 'plot' in Psalm 2:1b is the same word as 'meditate' in Psalm 1:2b. 'So these two introductory psalms set over against each other a quiet and continuous devotion to the teaching of the Lord as the way of righteousness and blessing in contrast to a vain and empty scheming against God's righteous rule'.[13] Psalm

2 is pragmatic about the opposition to the rule of Israel's king, just as Psalm 1 was utterly realistic in its recognition of the temptation not to follow the way of Yahweh's *torah*. The Psalter was probably 'published' in the post-exilic time,[14] when Israel was small and vulnerable among the great nations of the day. Indeed, Israel's history was one of vulnerability to great nations like Assyria and Babylon. At a time when religion and politics were inseparable, what sense did it make for other individuals, let alone nations, to pursue Yahweh's *torah*? Israel's international status proved that he was a 'weak and defeated god'.

In vv. 4ff, the scene moves to heaven. Here Yahweh is firmly on the throne! Yahweh laughs at his competitors and affirms the Israelite king as his deputy. This is an extraordinarily powerful relativization of all human power:

> In a strange way it is one of the most assuring sounds of the whole Psalter as it relativizes even the largest of human claims for ultimate control over the affairs of peoples and nations. The fiercest terror is made the object of laughter and derision and thus is rendered impotent to frighten those who hear the laughter of God in the background.[15]

Psalm 2 similarly ends on an extraordinary note (vv. 10–12); Yahweh is king and thus the rulers of the nations should follow the path of instruction and blessedness too!

> So as the introduction to the Psalter comes to a close we learn that this book will speak to us of individuals and their way and destiny but also of kings and nations and their conduct and fate. The righteous one before the law of the Lord and the rulers before the anointed of the Lord are

both in view. The modes and questions of individual conduct and the behavior of peoples and nations are matters of concern in these psalms. In the move from Psalm 1 to Psalm 2 the human plane is greatly expanded. If we have moved from a way the individual should walk to the rule of nations and empires, it is still the way of the Lord and the Lord's rule.[16]

This theme of the Lord's reign, or what the New Testament calls 'the kingdom of God',[17] is central to the Psalter. Psalms 72 and 89 are strategically placed royal psalms and Gordon Wenham's chapter explores the Psalms in the 90's that focus explicitly on this theme. The point of this theme is that, just as with the Lord's prayer – 'your kingdom come, your will be done' – we are to give ourselves over now to a life of blessedness, instructed by God, despite all the opposition to God's rule. Yahweh does reign – he is the one who laughs! – and he will reign. In the drawing at the start of the chapter this is the significance of the scroll. Even those waves that are unleashed upon us from time to time, are under God's control! History, symbolized by the unfolding scroll is ultimately His story. And despite all the evidence to the contrary we are to live in the light of this reality. The Psalter is there precisely in order to help us to live lives shaped from A-Z by Yahweh's instruction, amidst the reality of that in-between time of knowing that he reigns and seeing that he reigns.

This life of instruction and blessedness can never be confined to our private lives. It is quite clear from Psalm 2 that Yahweh's torah is as relevant to our individual lives as it is to the life of the nations. The whole of life comes from God, and if we are instructed by Yahweh, we will be keen to relate our faith to every aspect of our lives and of our societies. One of the great heresies of some twentieth-century Christianity has been a privatization of faith which will have nothing to do with the great areas of contemporary culture such as education, politics, art and commerce. The Psalms will have nothing to do with such a tendency. God is the King, and we need to take his royal reign seriously in all areas of life. That will not be easy, which is why we need the Psalms!

REFLECTION

- Are you surprised that the book of the Psalms introduces *the nations* in Psalm 2? Why?
- What according to Psalm 2, is it wise for the nations of the world to do? What do you think this means?
- Some people think that Christianity is about a personal faith which has nothing to do with politics, economics, education, and national issues. What does Psalm 2 teach us about this?

Pray the Lord's Prayer, reflecting in particular upon the petition,

'Your Kingdom Come,
Your rule be done,
on earth as it is in heaven.'

Questions/Activities

1. How do you feel about reading the Psalms as a book? What are the arguments for this?
2. Psalms 1 and 2 are the introduction to the Psalms. What issues do they alert us to at the outset of the Psalms?
3. Reflect on the drawing at the start of the chapter. How does this relate to the issues you identified in answer to question 2 above?
4. Reflect on the cover of the book. Do you find these issues there too?
5. If individuals and nations should seek God's instruction in all areas of life, where should we/they get this?
6. In what ways do Psalms 1 and 2 make you excited about getting in to the book of Psalms?

Notes

1. I think this phrase comes from Calvin, but I have been unable to track it down.
2. On this theme see Bartholomew and Moritz (eds.), *Christ and Consumerism: A Critical Analysis of the Spirit of the Age* (Carlisle; Paternoster, 2000).
3. Peterson, *Working the Angles*, 39
4. Most versions translate this name of God as the LORD. See Exodus 3 and 6 on this name of God.
5. J.C. McCann, *A Theological Introduction to the Book of Psalms: The Psalms as* Torah (Nashville: Abingdon, 1993), 28.
6. Ibid., 28.
7. Ibid., 30.
8. Ibid., 31.

9. L. Steele, *On the Way: A Practical Theology of Christian Formation* (Grand Rapids: Baker, 1990), 121.
10. Ibid., 35.
11. P. Miller, *Interpreting the Psalms*, 87.
12. Two other strategically placed royal psalms in the Psalter are Psalms 72 and 89.
13. Ibid., 89.
14. Israel went into exile in 587 BC in Babylon because of her continual disobedience to Yahweh. Some Israelites returned some 60 years later, but Israel never recovered her previous greatness.
15. Ibid., 90.
16. Ibid., 91.
17. See, for example, Mark 1:14,15. The kingdom of God/heaven is the main theme of Jesus' teaching.

The boat at the bottom of the scroll beckons us to embark on the journey set out in the Psalms. There is much about the journey that we do not know – not all the scroll is visible in the drawing. But the destination is clear – Mount Zion where God dwells!

'WHO MAY ASCEND THE HILL OF THE LORD?'

The Picture of the Faithful in Psalms 15–24

Gordon McConville

Psalms to read: Psalms 22, 23, 24

1. Longing for 'home'

Reading the Psalms

In Craig Bartholomew's chapter on Psalms 1–2, we saw how the Psalter has come, more and more, to be read as a book in which themes are developed from psalm to psalm, sometimes covering large portions of the whole book. This is probably not how most readers have read the Psalms, because they look on the surface like a collection of separate pieces. Yet it is clear that there are groups of Psalms, such as the run of 'hallelujah' psalms that close the Psalter (Psalms 146–150).[1] These allow the enormous range of experience expressed in the collection to end on a note of almost pure praise. Some such groups are overtly marked, for example by the five-book structure of the whole (see the Introduction), or by having similar headings (e.g. the 'Asaph' psalms, Psalms 73-83).[2] Others have to be discerned by attention to the recurrence of certain themes or expressions.

To read the psalms in this way does not mean that this is how they were originally written, but only that in the course of their use someone saw fit to gather them into their present order. Nor does identifying such groups mean that they are completely separate from the psalms around them. Links between groups can also be found. But as it seems that the compilers of the Psalter meant something by the way in which individual psalms are grouped, it is rewarding to try and retrace the theological themes that emerge from studying them in this way.

Psalms 15–24

In this chapter, I want to consider Psalms 15–24. This group has been taken as a self-contained section by a number of writers.[3] One reason for this is that Psalms 15 and 24 share a theme, namely the question who is worthy to ascend, or dwell on, the 'hill of the LORD'? Mount Zion in Jerusalem is, of course, the 'hill of the LORD'; it is the place where the temple stood. So, these psalms, which are sometimes called 'entrance liturgies', portray the righteous person, the one who is qualified to participate in worship. For that reason they continue the theme that was introduced in Psalms 1–2: the bringing of all life under God's teaching or instruction (see chapter 1). The celebration of this Torah is raised again in another psalm in our group, Psalm 19.

Psalms 15–24 are also unified by a further theme, namely a sense of being, or longing to be, 'at home'. The 'home' language appears right at the beginning: 'O LORD, who may *dwell* in your sanctuary? Who may *live* on your holy hill?' (15:1). It returns near the end of the group, when the psalmist knows that he will 'dwell in the house of the LORD for ever' (23:6). In these verses, 'home' is defined as being in the presence of God. To translate it into other idioms, we may recall St. Augustine's famous confession: 'My heart is restless till it find its rest in Thee'. Perhaps all deep longing is really a yearning for God, even if it is not always recognized as such.[4] Longing can be agonizing, especially if there is no confidence in the possibility of it being fulfilled. It is, perhaps, not surprising that the language of 'home' recurs in passages that speak of being with God (e.g. John 14:2).

We will notice, in Psalms 15–24, a progression from longing to rest. In between, we will go with the psalmists into the depths, as in the story of Passion to Easter. This too is a story of Passion to Easter. Who is the subject of it? In one sense it is King David. In another it is Jesus Christ. Yet, as we shall see, the journey expressed in these psalms may take place in the life of any one of us.

2. The *Narrative* in these Psalms

We begin with a quick sweep through the group of psalms, to try to bring out a kind of narrative progression in which the godly, righteous person is the central character.

Psalm 15

Psalm 15 sets the scene. It gives a schematic picture of the righteous person, who has a home with the LORD in his 'sanctuary' (literally 'tent', with its echo of the tabernacle in the time of Israel's wilderness wanderings). The 'dwelling', correspondingly, is a kind of sojourning, the temporary residence of a stranger. The second part of the line ('Who may live on your holy hill?') brings a progression, however. The 'tent' is now the 'holy hill' of Mount Zion. The opening line, therefore, has a reminiscence of the movement from the tabernacle in the wilderness to the temple in Jerusalem. The movement may also correspond to a context of pilgrimage, in which the psalmist anticipates arriving at the place of worship, along with a host of other worshippers (as in Psalm 84).

This psalm may have been a confession in a liturgy on some great occasion. The qualities required in the worshipper are representative of the ethical standards expressed in various parts of the Old Testament, especially in the Ten Commandments (Exodus 20:1–17), and such places as Job 31. Surprisingly, the stress on speech is often brought out in summary statements of right and wrong behaviour (cf. Jeremiah 9:2–9; Psalm 12:1-4; James 3:1–12). At its heart is the power of speech to bring either harmony or cause great damage in a community. The vision, therefore, is the joining together of the faithful in harmony in the presence of God, not a righteous person in isolation.

REFLECTION

The illustration that goes with this chapter shows a temple at the top of a hill, recalling the pilgrimage to Jerusalem. But the picture of it is stylized, and suggests that life itself is a pilgrimage. Consider:

1. How the life of faith is a difficult upward progression and a journey 'home'.
2. The ways we might, or actually do, go as a people together on the journey of faith?

Pray for the church family that you are a member of as you journey together with God.

Psalm 16

In Psalm 16 the righteous person chooses the LORD (vv. 1–2, 5), in contrast to those who choose other gods (v. 4). Consequently, she know the blessings God gives: his presence, counsel and deliverance from death are boundary lines that have fallen 'in pleasant places' (vv. 6–10), which is a delightful way of expressing contentment with a life that has known blessing and joy.

The psalmist, however, is apparently in some danger because she seeks refuge in the LORD (v. 1). This may bring in a slightly disturbing element, but it also turns the attention from the specific situation of worship back to the regular situations of life – there is a focus on the 'land' (v. 3) and the LORD's presence 'at night' (where 'night' evokes both danger and regularity). The LORD is present in all times and places and not just in the temple. There is, however, a link between these two kinds of presence because the climax of the psalm is joy, which is found at home (probably the temple) in the presence of the LORD (v. 11).

Psalm 17

If the idea of refuge in Psalm 16 introduced a disturbing note, Psalm 17 increases the profile of enemies and potential harm. As the psalm opens, the psalmist feels the need of deliverance from some danger, which involves slander (vv. 1–2), and pleads fervently for vindication (vv. 3-8). The threat of the enemies is depicted vividly (vv. 9–12). The worshipper pleads for his innocence to be known and his enemies to be defeated (v. 13). The climax again comes in his being in the presence of God. The phrases 'I shall see your face', and 'seeing your likeness' (v. 15), are ways of expressing being with the LORD, probably in the temple. The connection here, as in Psalm 15, between this closeness to God and *righteousness* (vv. 1, 15) is clear.

Psalm 18

This psalm brings a real struggle. The psalmist's enemies are, again, the source of the trouble (v. 17); the psalmist uses the strongest language yet to express this fear. The dominant image for the danger he experiences is that of the depths of the ocean (vv. 4, 16), which often stands for the forces of chaos that stand in opposition to the ordering and creating power of God. However, the psalmist's salvation is never in doubt; the Psalm is an account of how the LORD saved him from the great threat (vv. 1–3, 6–24). Indeed, it demonstrates the LORD's power to re-create order in the life of the believer, because he controls the forces of creation itself. It might be said that God *moves heaven and earth* to rescue the psalmist (vv. 7–15, 16–17). This cosmic imagery, picturing tottering mountains, smoke and fire, the sky and the wind, darkness and light, lightning and penetration to the heart of the oceans, lays claim to the creation for the LORD. God can 'reach down from on high' (v. 16) because of this and is able to deliver the psalmist from danger, to a 'spacious place' (v. 19, cf. 16:6, 'pleasant places').

The location of the LORD in *his temple* (v. 6) is not out of keeping with this vision of the LORD ruling over the elements, because it is a symbol of his kingship in the whole world. At the same time, it recalls the psalmist's desire to be with God, the temple being the place of pilgrimage and longed-for rest (Psalm 15). The psalmist's innocence (or righteousness) is, correspondingly, restated (vv. 20–24), together with the dependability of the LORD to respond to people in good measure (vv. 25–30).

The psalm now takes a turn (v. 31), and the last twenty verses celebrate the psalmist's defeat of enemies, thanks to the LORD's help. The language is distinctly military – these enemies are no mere mockers – and the reason becomes clear in the last two verses, where the theme of victory over enemies is placed in the context of the life of David and of God's promise to him (2 Samuel 7:11–17). It was, of course, announced as such by the heading, which declares that David composed the psalm on the day of his deliverance from his enemies, especially Saul. A further pointer to David in this connection is that Psalm 18 also appears, virtually verbatim, in 2 Samuel 22, in that book's closing reflection on God's faithfulness to David throughout his life. That David is in some sense the subject of the psalms before us, therefore, is nowhere clearer than at this point. Here he is also termed God's 'anointed' (or 'Messiah', v. 50). In our meditative reading we are therefore pointed to new levels of meaning (to which we will return). In terms of the developing theme, however, we notice primarily the LORD's capacity to save his faithful one.

Psalm 19

In Psalm 18 we saw a close relationship between God's control of the forces of all creation and his love and care for the psalmist. Now the heavens themselves declare God's handiwork (19:1-4). This is one of the most beautiful and direct expressions in the Bible of the idea that the splendour of the creation itself is a pointer to God. To the eye of faith at least, the heavens are an open book, leading the mind and spirit to their author. In our generation we have been able to instruct our natural human amazement at the universe with an array of technical knowledge unavailable to any before us. Yet, the more we know the more the measure of the universe eludes us. Often those who delve most deeply into the diversities of the world we live in – immeasurable both in grandeur and minuteness, with their fantastic interrelationships and causalities – express the most wonder (though, it must be said, not always).

The universe is portrayed here as *instruction*. The theme of speech, which we noticed in Psalm 15, is returned to here ('speech', 'knowledge', 'language', 'voice'). As in Psalm 15 it is true speech, but now it is speech of the LORD. In the striking way in which it is used, a similarity is declared between the disclosures of God in his *word* and in his creation. This explains the sudden transition in verse 7 to the theme, once again, of Torah. God who is known in his works is also known in his word. God who creates in power beyond imagining is the righteous God who seeks the faith of believers. It is good to desire and pursue the Torah because it conforms to the way the universe truly is.[5]

REFLECTION

In the illustration, the journey is pictured as beginning with Noah's ark settled on its peak, the flood behind, having set the children of Noah on the path of life and faith. The scroll-shape of 'Ararat' hints that the way to life is one of obedience. The journey begins with life-giving command and ends with a homecoming in God's presence. How does Psalm 18 teach us to face the 'storms' of life? What does Psalm 19 make us think about the 'law' of God?

FOR PRAYER:

I love you, O Lord, my strength,
Who reached down from on high and drew me up.
Who turns my darkness into light.
Whose glory is declared in the heavens
And who give precious and sweet laws
To teach me the way to God.
I love you, O Lord, my strength.

Psalms 20–21

The Davidic-Messianic note is struck in Psalm 20:6. Psalm 20 is a prayer for the king's triumph over his enemies. The scene of the prayer may be the temple; certainly the temple is in the centre of the picture, in which the LORD is asked to send help from the 'sanctuary', and 'Zion'. The prayer for the king in this context recalls the special place King David had in the covenant between the LORD and Israel. In his promise to David, God had undertaken to be faithful to David and his descendants 'for ever' (2 Samuel 7:13). In the security thus extended to the king the people are blessed too (notice how the 'we' comes into the prayer here, vv. 5, 8), an important aspect of the Messianic idea. The prayer here is based on this promise and the temple is also a sign of it.

Thematically, the psalm follows on well from the reminiscence of David in Psalm 18 – there is, perhaps, even an echo of the young shepherd's triumph, in vulnerability, over the well-armed Philistine giant (vv. 6-7; cf. 1 Samuel 17:37, 47). Psalm 21 continues the theme of the LORD's protection of his servant the king, who is in turn the model of a righteous person.

Psalm 22

This psalm brings a low point in the psalmist's experience, with its famous opening words, taken by Jesus on the cross: 'My God, my God, why have you forsaken me?' The theme of forsakenness identifies the psalm as a psalm of lament. It is not uncommon for the authors of these prayers to express a feeling that God is hidden from them (another example is Psalm 10). The sense of abandonment is perhaps more poignant here than anywhere else, the opening verse poetically conveys an anguished desolation.

There is, however, a turning point, as there often is in such Psalms. The desperate one turns again to God in petition (vv. 19–21), going on to praise God, calling others to do so as well, and foreseeing a turning of the world to God, now and in the future (vv. 27–30). Incidentally, this structure says much about the nature and the potential of prayer.

Psalms 23–24

The turning point in Psalm 22 leads on in the next two Psalms to restorations. The righteous person walks confidently, even in dark places, and knows that she will enjoy the presence of God, to the discomfiture of their enemies (Psalm 23). This group of psalms ends with a return to the opening theme: the righteous enter the place of God's dwelling and witness his triumphant possession of the whole earth, which is rightfully his (Ps. 24).

These final three psalms can be considered, helpfully, against the background of the life of King David. The mockery of the psalmist by enemies (v. 7) recalls David being humiliated by the insults of Shimei – a relation of the defeated former king, Saul – as he fled Jerusalem during the rebellion of his son, Absalom (2 Samuel 16:5-8). There are echoes too of David's earlier flight from Saul, when the boorish Nabal scornfully mocks David's servants (1 Samuel 25:10-11). The graphic images of illness and encirclement by ill wishers (vv. 14–18) might be the hyperbolic expressions of one who feels desperate in persecution.

David is, in due course, restored to his kingdom: he might well have reflected, in his old age, on the goodness of the LORD who delivered him from many dangers (22:21; 23) and who dwelt finally in the 'house of the LORD' (23:6). He may even have presiding over the great liturgy celebrating his kingship (Psalm 24).

We shall return to Psalms 22–24 below, but first it is time to reflect further on who is the subject of these songs.

REFLECTION

- In Psalms 20–24, there are a series of 'turnings', or ups and downs. Pick these out, then ask: What part does prayer play in the life of the faithful?
- Use these thoughts to shape your own prayerful response to God.

3. A story of David's 'greater son'

We shall return to Psalms 22–24 below, but first it is time to reflect further on who is the subject of these songs. Christians have read the psalms with reference to Jesus Christ since the earliest times. The New Testament's attributions of Old Testament texts to him are at the root of this. He is the 'son of David' (Matthew 1:1; 21:9) who comes to fulfil the promises made to his illustrious ancestor, the 'anointed one' ('Messiah'; Matthew 23:10; John 4:25–26) who is also 'suffering servant' (Matthew 20:28; Philippians 2:7-8). This does not mean that the psalms were always intended, literally and exclusively, to refer to the events told in the sacred narratives, whether in the Old or New Testaments. Even the reference of the psalms to David, as we have noticed, is no doubt the fruit of reflection by worshipping communities on the life of that king. The inclusion of Psalm 18 in the Psalter and in 2 Samuel 22 is evidence of this reflection (though Psalm 18 may indeed be a psalm of David). The same is true of readings of the psalms in the light of Jesus' life and sufferings.

Indeed, the possibility of reading the psalms in the light of the lives of David and Jesus arises, paradoxically, from their universality. The themes of this group of psalms are certainly universal: the tension between the expected reward of the righteous in blessing and the disturbing facts of life, in which these expectations are not always fulfilled, the righteous person's desire to be at home with God and her belief that it will be so in the end. The psalms are in this respect not far from the book of Job.

The psalms can be readily applied to Christ because of their capacity to reach into the deepest parts of human experience. To put it differently, Jesus felt drawn to them – they were a powerful way of expressing his agony – for this reason his use of Psalm 22 is extremely thought provoking. At one level the cry 'My God, my God, why have you forsaken me?' is only what might be expected from a man in extreme pain and on the brink of death. Yet, when we question these words of Jesus further, we find that they are as impenetrable as the being of the Incarnate One, the God-man. The emotions that the psalms express may be humanly universal, but how can humans understand them when God appropriates them in human flesh? What can we know of Jesus' state of mind in that hour? Only that the sense of dereliction, which all may know, must be compounded out of all knowing by who he was. Who may ascend the hill of the LORD? One who has clean hands and a pure heart. Well, here he is; the one who does these things and embodies them – mocked, humiliated and crucified by those who were blind to him. This is Gethsemane writ large. The suffering of the servant is shown to all but is by its nature, hidden.

Here, then, is one sense in which the words spoken by Jesus say more than they appear to. But there is another because the words do not come newly minted from Jesus' lips. We cannot hear him utter them without recalling that he knew the Scriptures. If Jesus knew these opening words of the psalm, he would also have known how it continued. In expressing forsakenness, did Jesus not know that restoration lay beyond? In uttering the one line he, perhaps, meant to indicate the whole movement of the psalm. Certainly, the expressions of despair in the psalm lie close to the petitions for help: 'But you, O Lord, be not far off; O my Strength, come quickly to help me' (v. 19; cf. vv. 20–21). The declarations that the psalmist will testify to faithfulness of the LORD, who has heard his prayer (v. 22–24) and that there will be true worship and righteousness in the land, indeed in the world (vv. 26–31), are also close. It is hard to attribute pure forsakenness to Jesus. Did his cry of dereliction bear this vision of salvation? Was he driven by his vocation to save the world, even in the darkest hour?

Even so, we can only be cautious about this second point because of the first. If we cannot plumb the depths of Jesus' experience we cannot go on to say with certainty that he must have known the good outcome. The dereliction cannot be diminished, because it is a fact of his experience and the very one that he voices.

At this point Jesus' experience becomes universal again – we cannot even recognize it without our own fears coming into play. On the cross, Christ takes on the fullness and depth of human experience: not just terrible pain, but the fear of *finally* not belonging, the fear that truth and justice will not prevail, that mockery, arrogance, inhumanity will come out on top. Alongside this is the bittersweet hope that there will be joy beyond the turmoil of life.

REFLECTION

- How does Christ's experience of dereliction on the cross help us comprehend our own darkest moments? What do we cry out then?
- Pray for those known to you who are passing through a time of darkness.

4. Restorations

Now that we have seen that the messianic interpretation of the Psalms does not rule out their application to the lives of all readers, we focus finally on some moments in the movement through these last three psalms in this collection which express a spiritual trajectory that may be the experience of any human being.

Psalm 22

There is tremendous desolation here. It is embodied in the poetry itself. We feel the fainting anguish of verse 1. The agony of 'no answer', 'no silence' (i.e. 'rest', v. 2) sums up all agony. The elements in this desolation follow: he is scorned and outcast (vv. 6-8; 12–13, 16–18); faith itself is set at nought (v. 8); there is physical illness and exhaustion, to the point of death – and he is brought there by none other than God himself (vv. 14–15)! Here is 'Adam' undone, the human being with the life taken out, returning fast to the dust from which he was formed.

Also striking is the frantic switching between despair and prayer. Confidence is never far away, as we see from the 'yets' and 'buts' (vv. 3, 6, 9, 19). How true this is to the mixture of constancy and faithlessness that characterizes much believing.

There is a final turn to settled trust: ' … in the congregation I will praise you' (v. 22). There is no going back after this. This is 'home', and here is the essential movement of the psalm: from desolation to a place in the centre of the

worshipping community! Restoration in the psalms is gen-
erous, never grudging. We may recall how, in another place,
the penitent psalmist is not merely forgiven but restored to a
place of honour in which he 'teaches transgressors' (Psalm
51:13). Measures of grace are in such restorations.

There is an epilogue to the struggle: 'For he has not
despised or disdained the suffering of the afflicted one; he
has not hidden his face from him, but has listened to his cry
for help' (v. 24).

Psalm 23

We now enter a new landscape. Here all is calm – and familiar! The first line says all: *It is the LORD* who is my shepherd.
He is not some tyrant, or one of those false 'shepherds'
accused by prophets: 'Woe to the shepherds who are
destroying and scattering the sheep of my pasture…!' (Jeremiah 23:1–2). Neither is he one of those shepherds who fail
to guard the sheep because they have no love for them (John
10:12–13). The second part of the first line, 'I will lack nothing', assures us of this and implies a 'therefore'. Since the
LORD is my shepherd I cannot ultimately lack anything
important. There is an echo of the longing, which was our
opening theme: 'Who may dwell in your sanctuary?'

The imagery of this idyll is remarkable in Palestine: green
pastures and flowing water are the symbols of life. These
'quiet waters' are literally 'water of rest(s)/resting', that is,
water to linger beside because it gives a sense of peace. The
'quiet' water is surely flowing. It is a curiosity of water that
its perpetual movement conveys peace – as on a shore with

crashing breakers, or in a fountain; these are paradoxes of flux and deep stability. It is a perfect picture of the possibility of rest in the midst of turbulence. This 'rest' is nothing less than salvation: it is journey's end (cf. Deuteronomy 12:9–10), beyond war and striving. It is the knowledge now that the last word is one of wholeness, and the fulfilment of the longing.

The dark side is barely noticed here (v. 4); it is still there, but there is a frame of mind that can carry the faithful one through. The LORD as shepherd is there, knowing the pitfalls, doing the seeing when the believer gropes in the dark, and guiding her to a smooth, light place.

Then there is the banquet – and surprisingly, the enemies are here! The irony is delicious. Their mockery is reduced to silence. The words spoken in spiteful scorn (Psalm 22:8) turn out to be true! Those who bitterly enjoyed the upper hand are powerless here, in this true vision of reality, seeing the salvation of the faithful one who comes home!

Psalm 24

What more is to be said? The Shepherd you and I call 'ours', 'mine', is the King of Glory!

In verse 3, Psalm 24 returns to the question of Psalm 15, but the point is made more succinctly. It is sandwiched now between celebrations of the LORD as creator and ruler of the world. Here is the big picture. (It was there in Psalm 22 also, when the witness of the redeemed one 'in the congregation' (Psalm 22:22) meant that the whole world turned to the LORD: 'dominion belongs to the LORD ' (Ps. 22:27–28) in all time and everywhere. Now we have the grand climactic statement of the theme.

The earth is the LORD's (vv. 1–2) and he is coming to demonstrate his rule in it (vv. 7–8). There are two poles here that seem worlds apart: On one hand, a 'small corner' of an event: faithful people coming to worship the LORD in a temple in a city that only briefly had the status of an independent capital, and finding their God there; on the other, God's entry in glory into his kingship over the entire world. The connection between these things is staggering. What kind of order exists in the world and universe? The answer of the psalms is that there is only one, God's – and it is 'joined up government', that is, there is a connection between the moral 'order' that we are called into, which is represented by the Torah (his teaching and commands, always to be freshly heard and understood in each new generation), and the natural 'order' (not in some direct way, otherwise we slip into the error of Job's friends). There is a connection because there is nothing arbitrary or trivial about the commands of God, he is the creator of the universe and wisdom, and the source of all life.

Who may find their home in the tent of the LORD? Those who hold to the commands of the LORD in faithfulness – they believe that God can overcome every dark thing; he will lead them by the waters of life forever.

REFLECTION

- The way pictured in the illustration appears hard, yet we may pick out, or imagine, quiet stretches. Do you see the periods of peace and blessing as promises of God's final word of life to us?
- Use Psalm 23 as a prayer.

Questions/Activities

1. What might it mean in our experience to 'ascend the hill of the LORD' (Ps. 24:3)?
2. What are the marks of the righteous person, according to Psalms 15, 24?
3. What may we expect from prayer in times of distress (Psalms 18, 22)?
4. What are the elements in a rediscovery of joy?
5. What is added to an appreciation of these psalms by identifying the subject as King David, Jesus Christ or oneself?
6. Does Jesus' use of Psalm 22 teach us anything about how we might use the Bible? What does it teach us about his experience?

Notes

1. Andrew West considers these in chapter 5 of this volume.
2. See Jamie Grant's discussion of these psalms in chapter 3.
3. For example, P.D. Miller, 'Kingship, Torah Obedience, and Prayer', in K. Seybold and E. Zenger (eds.), *Neue Wege der Psalmenforschung* (Freiburg: Herder, 1995), 127-42. This essay provides a theoretical basis for some of the directions taken here.
4. This deep longing is well conveyed by the German term *Sehnsucht* and is a theme of much poetry that may be called Romantic.
5. See chapter 1 where Craig Bartholomew also explores the link between creation and Torah.

The closed scroll (here symbolizing history rather than the book of the Psalms) and the unlit candle remind us that we sometimes face dark and mysterious times in our journey with God.

PSALMS 73 & 89 –
THE CRISIS OF FAITH!

Jamie Grant

Psalms to read: Psalms 73 and 89

I sometimes wonder when it was that the contemporary church became perfect. When was it that we stopped being weak and fallible? When did we become self-sufficient? When was it that our lives and circumstances became manageable? Did I miss something? Did somebody finally discover the 'secret' to the successful Christian life and from that time on we have never had a problem in our walk with God? Have we never had a problem in our relationship with the world? Have we never had any difficulty in deciding right from wrong? Does the church, do Christians, no longer *have* crises of faith?

A further question: if the church has suddenly and amazingly become perfect, why do we not see the fruits of that perfection in our public worship, in our relationships with one another, in our witness and in our daily walk of faith?

Surely, if we are to be honest, we must admit that our Christian walk – both individual and corporate – is far from perfect. Truthfully, we *do* have doubts. We *are* sometimes afraid of present circumstance or future prospect. There *are* days when we do not understand why our life has taken this turn or that turn, and we are troubled by it. Sometimes it is easier for us to *speak* of the sovereignty of God than it is for us to *submit* to it.

A final question by way of introduction then: if the church is not perfect and if we really do experience crises of faith, *why then has the contemporary church turned its back on the psalms of lament?*

Psalms 73 and 89 are both honest expressions of how the psalmists feel and think when they come before God. There is no pretence, no façade. In today's church we have somehow developed the idea that we must always be 'up-beat' if we are true Christians. Always smiling and positive, that is the way we often feel obliged to present ourselves – regardless of how we really feel. This is an attitude unknown to the writers of the psalms, for psalms of lament are also known as *Psalms of Complaint*: individual and corporate complaint. This description is a fair reflection of the content which we can expect to find in the lament psalms. This honest expression of confusion and spiritual disorientation before God is, however, a far cry from the moaning and complaining for which, for example, the Israelites were punished in the wilderness.

Praises are written out of a desire to praise. Torah psalms are written out of love for the LORD and his word. However, crises of faith are real, and they too find their expression in the Psalms.

1. Psalms 73 and 89 in Context

Book 3 of the Psalter begins with Psalms 73 – a psalm of individual crisis – and ends with Psalm 89 – a psalm of public, national crisis. They echo the dual themes of the introduction to the Psalter.[1] If we continue being honest with ourselves, we will admit that we are all too able to relate to the psalmists' expressions in both of these psalms.

Which one of us has never looked at our own situation and despaired just a little? Who can claim to never having had a jealous thought towards those better off than ourselves? Which of us has never watched the news and thought in our hearts, 'What on earth is going on in this world?' Can we not relate *all too well* to the crises of Asaph and Ethan the Ezrahite?

The English name that we use for this collection of poems and songs is, of course, the book of *Psalms* (or the Psalter). This name is derived from the Greek and Latin translations of the Old Testament. The original Hebrew name for this book is slightly different: it is called the book of *Praises*. In some ways this is an odd name for a book that contains more psalms of *lament* than any other kind of psalm! Yet, this was the title that was chosen to describe the final form of the book, chosen for the book as a whole. This appears to be a strong point of tension, but in reality the road from lament to praise is not so far.

REFLECTION

- Do you feel under pressure always to be 'happy and up-beat' in your church?
- In what ways can you relate to the expressions of doubt expressed in Psalms 73 and 89?
- When you pray, do you believe that you can be 100% honest before God? Consider honestly and openly your state of being and how you see the world around about you – bring your thoughts to God in prayer.

A PRAYER:

'My flesh and my heart may fail, but God is the strength of my heart and my portion forever' (Psalm 73:26).

Thank you, Lord,
that I can be honest with you
about my doubts and weaknesses.
Thank you also that trust in you is never misplaced.
Give me eyes of faith to see as you would have me see.
Amen.

2. The Art of Asking Hard Questions

This is the real essence of the psalms of lament: they are poetic expressions of hard questions that deal with daily reality. The poet who wrote Psalm 73 tells us of the hard question he felt he had to ask. He then gives us an answer, which was revealed to him as a wave of dawning realization when he came to worship God.[2] Psalm 89 just asks the hard question. The psalmist did not *see* the answer to their dilemma, but that does not mean that they did not receive assurance (Ps. 89:52).

I suppose that two of the key questions that we have in relation to the laments are:

- Why are they in the Bible?
- How can we make use of them today?

The laments are found in the Bible because Scripture deals with the totality of covenant life and experience. In many ways the Bible is simply the account of God's dealings with humankind – creation, fall, redemption and renewal. In each of these aspects we see the Creator entering into *covenant* relationship with his people[3] – a relationship that is binding on both parties. This relationship therefore leads to certain expectations from either party.

There are many accounts in the Bible of occasions when *we* fail. Take, for example, the Israelites in the desert, their covenant unfaithfulness led to punishment – God's justice poured out in response to breach of promise.[4] Breach of covenant is not something to be brushed under the carpet. There is always a sense in which it is something to be dealt with openly, honestly and without delay. Covenant is important, we can't just forget about it.

That is exactly the point of the psalmists who wrote the psalms of lament! Covenant is binding upon both parties, and in the psalms of lament the psalmist is honestly and openly expressing what he sees to be a breach of covenant on *God's* part. Yahweh makes promises as he graciously enters into relationship with his people. This is almost too amazing for our minds to grasp, but the Almighty Creator of the universe, binds himself to a certain type of relationship with his people, to a certain type of relationship with us! He makes promises, and in the laments the psalmists are secure enough in their knowledge of who God is and what he is like, to be able to say: 'But what about this? Didn't you make a promise to us? I don't see you keeping that promise!'

It sounds almost irreverent, but it is not. Such are the depths of relationship that God calls us to enter into – a bond so deep that we can be entirely honest. A bond where we can say (in all humility and with the awareness that we often are wrong), 'LORD, that's not fair!' Pious dishonesty is not something that God desires from us. It makes no sense to say to the One who sees all and knows all, 'I'm fine,' when in reality our hearts are breaking. Or to declare that, 'I will sing of your love forever,' when we are none too sure if he does love us or even if he is really there, due to the suffering which we may be experiencing at the present time. Such emptiness is not the *covenant* relationship that God has called us to enter into in Christ Jesus. Covenant relationship means that we *can* cry out and say, 'But, LORD God, you promised …'

REFLECTION

- Look through the Psalter and meditate upon some of the promises that God has made to his people.
- Look at the picture at the front of this chapter and focus on the candle which is no longer burning.
- What are the implications of being in a covenant relationship with God?
- Ask yourself the question, 'Am I content with the intimacy of my walk with God? Is my relationship with Him growing deeper or have I lost something of the closeness of walk that I once had?'

A PRAYER:

'But as for me, it is good to be near God' (Psalm 73:28)

Help me, Father God,
to walk in your paths
and to live more fully for you every day.
Amen.

3. Problems of Perspective

The lament psalms are all about perspective – the psalmist's
and ours. They pronounce that *from our perspective* it appears
God has broken his side of the agreement. That is the way
we feel, that is the way we see things and God wants to hear
the honest expression of our hearts. Pious words will not
fool him because he sees the attitude of our hearts.

Our problem, however, is one of *perspective* when it
comes to judging covenant unfaithfulness. We are often
mistaken. It's that simple. Yahweh's perspective is perfect –
he knows when we have been unfaithful. Our view on
things is far from perfect, which is one of the lessons of
Psalm 73.

Surely we can all relate to Asaph's dilemma. Psalm 1
makes the reality of spiritual life quite clear. There are two
ways: the way of the wicked leading to death (Psalm 1:1, 4–
6) and the way of the 'blessed' leading to life (Psalm 1:2–3,
6a). The call of Psalm 1, which (together with Psalm 2) is
really the paradigm for reading the whole of the Psalter, is
quite straightforward. 'Delight in God's instruction, walk in
his ways and everything will be alright.' Justice will be done
– life for those who walk with God and death for the
wicked.[5]

But Asaph has a problem; he sees the wicked prosper!
This doesn't fit within his Psalm 1 paradigm of how life
should be. Take a look at verses 4–11. These people, the
objects of Asaph's consideration, are proud, violent, hard-
hearted, sinful and arrogant; what's more, they even dare to
defy God (Psalm 73:11)! Yet, they prosper (vv. 3–5, 12)!

How can this be? Surely this does not square with the promise of Yahweh to his people. This must be covenant unfaithfulness on *God's* part, or so Asaph thinks at first.

We see his loss of perspective in the verses of Psalm 73. 'They have no struggles …' – I wonder if the people observed by Asaph would have said the same thing? 'Always carefree, they increase in wealth …' – if we could see into their hearts, would that be the reality or merely the façade? However, this loss of perspective affected Asaph deeply, shaking his understanding of the spiritual and, indeed, the everyday reality of his walk with God. He declares, 'Surely, in vain have I kept my heart pure … I have been plagued … I have been punished' (vv. 13-14). How often have we, at the very least, been tempted to think like that? Sometimes – from *our* perspective – it just seems that it is simply not worth being a Christian! Too much sacrifice on our part and everyone else seems to be much better off! But we too can experience problems of perspective.

It had all become too much for Asaph (v. 16) until he started to see things from a different perspective, i.e. God's eternal perspective – 'till I entered the sanctuary of God' (v. 17). It is amazing how different everything appears from another perspective. Look at a handmade Persian rug from underneath and we see nothing but a mass of brightly coloured threads going this way and that without any apparent sense of design or reason. We can only see the beauty and plan of the rug – the pattern of the designer – when we look at it from above. It was when Asaph came before the LORD that the rug was flipped over for him to catch a glimpse of the design.

We are not told what Asaph did in the sanctuary. Did he pray? Was it the sermon that spoke to him? Was it the public reading of the Scriptures? We don't know exactly. But we know that Asaph met with God. He did business with God and he realized his folly. He realized that Yahweh's promise of blessing did not necessarily mean an easy life for the believer, but it did mean an eternal life (v. 24). He came to know afresh that the wicked may prosper now, but the way of the wicked still *ultimately* leads to death (vv. 17b–20) – most of all, Asaph saw that really *he*, and not the wicked, was the truly rich man. What treasures can they offer to compare with the friendship of God, his protection, his counsel and eternal security (vv. 22–23)? He came to know a contentment that the 'rich, carefree wicked' would never know – 'But as for me, it is good to be near God' (v. 28).

Does this mean that his complaint was illegitimate or inappropriate? I think not. Would he ever have learnt the lesson if he had not voiced the complaint? Besides which, imagine how much deeper Asaph's praise of the living God would be, from this point of renewed relationship with Yahweh. Yes, we can all offer lip praise whilst thinking about something else entirely and never ask any hard questions. Asaph offers new depths praise because he opened his heart in honesty before God, and the LORD met with him.

We do not know what happened to Asaph in the sanctuary, but this pivotal verse (v. 17) does teach us one important lesson. We need to submit ourselves regularly to the means of grace. Are we reading the Word individually and meditating upon it (Psalm 1)? Are we praying to God that he should help us and change us, crying out as the psalmists did? Are we coming together to worship, pray, study the Scriptures and to minister to one another? We must, because it is in these acts of faith that *our perspectives are transformed* (Romans 12:1–2).

Psalm 89 expresses another problem of perspective. What about God's promise to David (the Davidic covenant)? David was not to build a house for God. Rather, God would build a house for David (i.e. a monarchic line).[6] Again the psalmist pours out his heart in all honesty. The covenant with David is broken and the psalmist cries out, 'How long, O LORD?' Just look at the impassioned plea laid out before God in verses 38-41.

We again see the problem of perspective. Ethan the Ezrahite could see the exile and the lack of a Davidic king, but he could not see 'Jesus Christ the son of David' (Matthew 1:1). The covenant was not broken; the stage was being set for it to enter into its ultimate fulfilment. Our perspective is limited; God's is not. Our point of view is tied up in time and space; God's is eternal and all encompassing. Hence, sometimes we feel that we must cry out in honest and humble complaint because from our perspective it just seems wrong! Even as we do so, just as Ethan did, we need to remind ourselves of the amazing character of our Heavenly Father and of his loving hand controlling every area of our lives and of history.

REFLECTION

- Have there been times when your perspective on life became skewed? How did that affect you? What helped you to renew a right perspective?
- Meditate upon Psalm 73:22–23. Think about all the riches that the believer has as a result of relationship with God through Christ.
- Look at the picture and think about the closed scroll.
- Do you, for example, regularly practise prayer, bible reading/meditation and join in public church worship? These things are important if we are to maintain the right perspective on life and eternity.

A PRAYER:

'Whom have I in heaven but you? And earth has nothing I desire besides you?' (Psalm 73:25).

Thank you Lord, for the amazing riches that come from being your child.

May my heart be more and more consumed with the desire to live to please you day-by-day.

Amen.

4. The Legitimacy of the Lament Psalms

Does this mean that we should not express our laments and complaints? Is it right that the church has rejected the psalms of lament? Perhaps, our outward appearance of 'fineness' really is the way forward? Again, I think not, for several reasons.

Canon

We cannot pass-off the lament psalms as a Semitic peculiarity and therefore ignore them. The laments make up a large part of the Psalter – Gunkel highlights 39 psalms of individual lament and 19 psalms of corporate lament, not to mention passages from Jeremiah, Job and the book of Lamentations! To ignore the laments is to cut out a large chunk of the Bible. Obviously, this is something that is significant to our theological understanding of God. What lesson does this teach us? It appears that one of the key emphases of the lament psalms is *the reality and intimacy of our relationship with God*. What was it that Asaph learnt from his complaint? 'It is good to be near God.' Look at the four power-packed sentences we find in Psalm 73:23–24:

> Yet I am always with you;
> you hold me by my right hand.
> You guide me by your counsel,
> and afterwards you will take me into glory.

They all focus on the closeness of Asaph's relationship with Yahweh! He realises that it is in this relationship that he finds his wealth and his purpose, and that regardless of circumstances the LORD will be his sufficiency. The complaint psalms seek, in essence, to deepen relationship with God. James L. Mays writes:

> 'A cry means something only in a created universe. If there is no creator, what is the good of calling attention to yourself?' (E.M. Cioran) ... The plea is addressed to the LORD, the creator of heaven and earth and of Israel. The psalm is language in which the desperate loneliness of human life is offered to God, who is its ultimate source and only final help. It is a prayer in which mortals in anxiety and anguish speak of themselves to God and in doing so speak *about* God to those of us who read the prayer as Scripture.[7]

These psalms are not just included for the sake of it, they have a prominent position in the Psalter. Clearly, as Mays points out, there are lessons to be learnt from the psalms of complaint. The record of Asaph's complaint and the answer that he received is designed to be of great encouragement to us, as we read his lament.

Dependence on God

The lament is in itself an open confession of our finite nature and therefore a submission of self to the sovereignty of God. Even in questioning Yahweh's covenant faithfulness, we acknowledge our inability and our total dependence on his capability. Asaph confesses his inability to comprehend the realities of life round about him. He could not cope (Psalm 73:15-16), but his complaint is not a rejection of God. Rather it is the opposite; he is throwing himself upon

God. He knew the character of his God (v. 1), but the problem vexed him and the question had to be asked. Asaph could not work it all out. The wealth and ease of the wicked troubled him, yet verse 15 shows us that he would not reject the way of God. Asaph's lament was not rebellion, but rather an expression of the depth and reality of the crisis of faith, which he was experiencing. It is like the small child, angry at his parent, who bangs his fists against his father's chest, yet at the same time does not wish to be released from his father's embrace. Somehow, even as he struggled with his complaint, Asaph knew that there must be an answer and that there could be only one source of that answer, hence his prayer of lament.

In Psalm 89 the psalmist does not come to Asaph's privileged position of understanding. His problem is not solved. Yet even in making his plea, he forcefully and clearly acknowledges that there is a God who makes sense of the world. There is a God who *does* care for his people –individually and corporately. The doxology at the end of Book 3 seems somewhat inappropriate in the light of the content of Psalm 89. Yet, in fact, it is most appropriate. The complaint is voiced (vv. 38-51). Held in tension with this lament, the character of God is known to the psalmist (vv. 1-37). Ethan knows that Yahweh is loving (vv. 1–2) and covenant-making (vv. 3-4). He is the awesome Creator (vv. 5–8) who rules in power (vv. 9-13) and does so with righteous and justice, blessing his people (vv. 14-18). What is more, Yahweh has revealed himself to his people in word and deed (vv. 19–29). Ethan does not receive an answer to his complaint. The tension, between the reality that he sees and the God whom he knows, still exists. The universal teaching of the Psalter is, however, univocal on this point – Yahweh reigns! Therefore, despite the fact that Ethan's lament remains unanswered, it is entirely appropriate that the last words of Psalm 89 and of Book 3 of the Psalms are:

'Praise be to the LORD for ever! Amen and Amen'
(Psalm 89:52).

Honesty before God

Why would God, 'who looks at the hearts of men' (1 Samuel 16:7), seek pious deceptions from us rather than an open expression of the honest truth? We in the church have fallen into habit of 'being fine.' We never really expect anyone to answer anything else to the question, 'How are you?' There is an accepted front of 'coping', which we present to the outside world whether we *really are coping* or not. Such well-intentioned falseness in our friendships becomes absolute folly in prayer. Our Creator and Redeemer seeks intimate relationship with his people – with us! So, what room is there for dishonesty in prayer? If our hearts are angry with God, does he not see that even though our words are polite? The God of covenant relationship would rather hear our anger and address it, than hear us deny the anger that he is all too well aware of. Prayer in covenant relationship must always be an exercise in honesty. All the more so since we have a high priest 'who has been tempted in every way, just as we are – yet was without sin' (Hebrews 4:15).

Change of Perspective

If our perspectives are wrong often it is in the expression of them that they are changed. Psalm 73 seems to be a case in point. Asaph was consumed with thoughts of betrayal. His heart was angry. He was sure that God had let him down. The rich were wealthy, he kept himself pure in vain – where was the promise of blessing of Psalms 1 & 2? We do not know whether Asaph expressed his complaint publicly before he had been led to see the answer, but we have every reason to believe that he expressed it to God. It was in meeting with God that Asaph discovered the truth.

In expressing our complaint, whilst submitting ourselves to the sovereignty of God at the same time, we open ourselves to be changed, corrected and learn the truth.

Ultimately, God does not want shallow praise based solely on words. He gladly receives deep praises, even those that are born out of a voiced complaint. We too can say, along with Psalm 89, 'I do not really know why all this has happened, but I know what my God is like'. Therefore

> '*Praise be to the LORD forever! Amen and Amen*'
> (Psalm 89:52).

5. Using Laments Today

So is it legitimate for us to make use of the lament psalms today? Do we still have crises of faith? If so, then we should use these psalms to express our own hearts in honesty, opening ourselves to correction. Of course, there will be many days when singing the psalms of praise and worship better expresses our hearts and minds. There will be days when things go wrong, when unanswerable crises arise; those are the days when the laments express our feelings better than anything else. Remember the goal of the laments: ever-deeper covenant relationship with God through the Son. There were times when psalms of lament best expressed Jesus' heart (Matthew 27:46), so should not his believers also be prepared to express our hearts in honesty before God?

Can we sing them?

We should also use the lament psalms in public worship to express our own corporate limitations and our dependence upon a sovereign God because the Church, as a body, also struggles. Politics and the state of the world at large depress and overwhelm us, morality appears to decline around about us and it is difficult to see the hand of God in the events of the day. Such is the context of the psalms of corporate lament. When the world and the wicked seem to be getting the upper hand, we need to pour out our hearts to God, just as the exilic and post-exilic Israelites did in Psalm 89. It is his world and he still reigns, so let us learn to give these things over to God in humility, allowing him to change and challenge our perspectives. Perhaps as we do begin to present these issues in sincerity before his throne we will begin to see his hand at work all the more in the world around us.

REFLECTION

- Do you skip over the lament psalms thinking them to be somehow 'less than Christian'? Instead, read them in the light of the psalmist's desire for deep and real relationship with God – what do we learn from them when read in this way?
- Consider the four reasons given above for the inclusion of the lament psalms. How are they reflected in your life?
- Think about appropriate ways of using the psalms of lament in your personal devotions and in services of public worship.

A PRAYER:

'How long, O Lord? Will you hide yourself for ever?' (Psalm 89:46).

Help me to be honest when I pray, Lord God.
Help me also to seek you every day of my life,
even when my heart is cold and I seem to be distant from you.
As a Good Shepherd, draw my heart near to you, I pray.
Amen.

6. Book 3 in Context

Book 3 of the Psalms is not the end of the story! One of the main themes of this series of articles is that we should read the psalms as a book. They are individual works, but they have been put together in a particular order to teach us lessons. Book 3 and Psalms 73 and 89 play a particular role in the story of the Psalter. Whilst there are many different psalms with a variety genres and contents in Book 3, the reader is left with the taste of lament in their mouth. 'What about the prosperous wicked? What about the Davidic covenant and the lack of a Davidic king? What is going on?'

The Psalter is not, however, finished with its Torah instruction. Psalm 73 has been highlighted as a theological centrepiece of the Psalter.[8] We start with the two ways of Psalms 1 and 2 – imbibe the Torah of Yahweh and live by it, reject the way of the wicked, follow his paths and blessing will be the result. Then comes the crisis of faith in Psalm 73 – the wicked prosper and the believer suffers in vain! This, however, is a crisis that has been resolved. Asaph sees the truth from an eternal perspective – blessing does not equal wealth, richness does not equal money and ease of life. Blessing is found in covenant friendship with the living God. Knowing your eternal security is true wealth. The wicked unbeliever has none of these things. The complaint is answered and the walk of faith is restored in Psalm 73. The two ways of Psalm 1 still apply, but the psalmist has come to a deeper understanding of this truth. So the reader can move from introduction (Psalms 1 & 2), to centrepiece (Psalm 73) and then conclusion (Psalm 150). The conclusion is simple:

'Let everything that has breath praise the LORD. Praise the LORD' (Psalm 150:6).

A deeper walk with God has been attained, and the praise that is offered in the end is a *deeper* praise. The result of the confrontation of the walk of faith with the reality of life still ultimately leads to honest praise because, although doubts may have been aired, the believer sees that Yahweh *is* always faithful to his covenant with his people.

Psalm 89 is another psalm in a key position for our understanding of the story of the Psalter. The psalmist and the people see no answer to their lament – at least the answer is not voiced in Psalm 89. The answer, to the crisis of Psalm 89, is, however, revealed to the *readers* of Book 4 of the Psalter! There may be no Davidic king at the moment, but Yahweh still reigns! That is the message of Book 4. God reigned in the times of Moses and he reigns through all times, even when David was king ultimately it was God who truly reigned! In many ways this is the central message of the Psalter. No matter what happens, *the LORD reigns!*[9]

The shadow of the Davidic king does make a reappearance in Books 4 and 5,[10] but with new, supernatural overtones! The book of Psalms ultimately points to a coming Davidic king who will fulfil the Torah of God and who will rule over the nations, as suggested by Psalms 1 and 2! That king has been revealed to us; hence, we can voice our crises of faith in submission and not rebellion. No matter how life may appear to us, the LORD still reigns in our lives and circumstances. God's Son intercedes for us at his right hand (Romans 8:34).

'Let us then approach the throne of grace with confidence, so that we may receive mercy and find grace to help us in our time of need' (Hebrews 4:16).

REFLECTION

- Think about the various lessons that you have learnt from this book thus far – what do the psalms of lament add to these lessons?
- 'The road from lament to praise in not so far.' Consider occasions when God has turned difficult circumstances into a cause for praise.
- *'The LORD reigns!'* Meditate upon the implications of this short statement both in terms of your life and your view of the world.

A PRAYER:

'Praise be to the Lord for ever! Amen and Amen!' (Psalm 89:52).

I praise you, Lord, because of your wonderful nature.
You do amazing deeds on our behalf.
Thank you that you never change
and that you reign over all things.
May this be a comforting thought
in days of doubt and difficulty.
Amen.

Questions/Activities

1. Discuss the issue of honesty in your church community.
   (a) Is everyone expected to be 'fine'?
   (b) Are you prepared to receive any other answer when you ask someone how they are?
   (c) How can we help one another to be honest and open enough to share how we really are?
2. How can the Scriptures help us when we face situations which are difficult to understand? (See chapters 1 and 2 about Psalms 1 and 19).

   Consider what the Psalms (especially the ones which we have studied so far) tell us about:
   (a) The character of God.
   (b) The promises which he has made to his people.
   (c) His control over history.
3. By what means do you seek to deepen your relationship with God?
   (a) What role does the reading of the Torah of God (the Bible) play in this process? Do we really study God's Word expecting to be challenged and changed? Individually? In small groups? As a church body?
   (b) What are your expectations when you attend church services? To be challenged and to grow in your walk with God?
   (c) Do you pray honestly and reverently before God? Or just 'as you think you ought'? Consider ways in which you can make your prayer life more honest.
4. Meditate upon and discuss the riches which you have as a believer. Use Psalm 73:23–24 as a guide.

5. Read and meditate upon Hebrews 4:14–16 and 7:23–24.
6. Consider how the High Priesthood of Jesus helps us to be honest before God and to go deeper into relationship with him (remember that the High Priest in the Old Testament acted as a mediator between the people and God).

Notes

1. We find a call to individual piety based upon delight in the Torah of Yahweh (Psalm 1) and a declaration of God's sovereign rule in every sphere of life (Psalm 2). Similarly, we find expression of individual crisis and national crisis at the beginning and end of Book 3 of the Psalms. See ch. 1 above.
2. Hence Psalm 73 is best described as a wisdom psalm. Its primary purpose is didactic, explaining a lesson learned, but this is a lesson born out of lament, as is acknowledged by H. Gunkel *Introduction to Psalms: The Genre of the Religious Lyric of Israel* (Macon: Mercer University Press, 1998), 299.
3. I would recommend O. Palmer Robertson, *Christ of the Covenants* (Presbyterian and Reformed: Philipsburg, NJ, 1980) and W. Dumbrell, *Covenant and Creation: An Old Testament Covenant Theology* (Paternoster: Exeter, 1984) as excellent treatments of the whole notion of 'covenant' in the Bible.
4. See Numbers 16 or 25 as examples of the harsh consequences of covenant unfaithfulness. The author of the book of Hebrews picks up on such examples as warnings to New Testament believers not to be tempted to turn away from true faith in Christ.
5. The term 'the wicked' has a somewhat different understanding in the Old Testament compared to our contemporary

usage of that term. It does not just refer to war criminals, murderers and the like. Rather, this idea of the wicked refers to all those who reject the Torah (instruction) of Yahweh and his rule over their lives.

6. 2 Samuel 7.

7. James L. Mays, *The LORD Reigns* (Louisville: Westminster John Knox Press, 1994), 55.

8. W. Brueggemann and P. D. Miller, "Psalm 73 as a Canonical Marker," *JSOT* 72 (1996) 45-56; J. C. McCann, "Psalm 73: A Microcosm of Old Testament Theology," in *The Listening Heart: Essays in Wisdom and Psalms in Honor of Roland E. Murphy* (eds. K. G. Hoglun, E. F. Huwiler, J. T. Glass, R. W. Lee; JSOTSup 58; Sheffield: JSOT Press, 1987) 247–257.

9. Hence, James Mays chose this as the title for his book. More on this topic will follow in the next chapter.

10. The prime example of this new 'super-king' would be Psalm 110.

The crown forms the apex of the triangle, speaking eloquently of God's kingship. The two horns of salvation (compare the cover) cross and are at rest beneath God's kingship. The tree in the centre signifies that this is where life and flourishing are truly to be found. The alpha and omega in the bottom corners of the triangle remind us that our King is the God of history and creation.

4

REJOICE THE LORD IS KING
Psalms 90–106 (Book 4)

Gordon Wenham

Psalms to read: Psalms 90 and 103

In the previous chapters we have looked at the first three
books of the Psalter (Ps 1–41, 42–72, 73 and 89). Now we
come to the fourth book, which consists of Psalms 90–106.
In our previous studies we have seen how the Psalter is
arranged like the Pentateuch in five books; the five books of
David's psalms echo the five books of Moses' law. Both are
books of *Torah* (i.e. divine instruction or law) that the righteous should meditate on day and night, if they wish to lead
a life that is blessed by God with success (Joshua 1: 7–8;
Psalm 1: 2–3).

We have noted that not all the psalms in the earlier books
are ascribed to David: some are anonymous; others are
ascribed to Levites such as Asaph and Korah. Most of the
psalms in the first three books would appear to have been
composed for use in the temple built by Solomon, but some
seem to be later works written after the destruction of that

temple by the Babylonians in 586 BC (e.g. Psalms 74, 89). That period is called the exile, for in 586 BC the majority of the Jerusalem elite were deported to Babylon, where they continued to practise their religion but with a sense of despair and guilt (cf. Psalm 137) for, as the prophets had told them, their exile had been caused by their own sinfulness (Isaiah 40:2; Ezekiel 18). Some fifty years after the fall of Jerusalem, Cyrus of Persia encouraged the Jews to return to Jerusalem and a few of them did (Ezra 1–2). They started to rebuild the temple, but soon gave up because things were so difficult (Haggai 1); it took the efforts of the prophets Haggai and Zechariah to persuade them to continue the rebuilding. We are told this second temple was much less impressive than the first; the returnees who had seen the first wept when they saw the second (Ezra 3:12). Indeed, in this post-exilic era things continued to be very difficult for the Jews. They faced food shortages, opposition from the Samaritans and it was another seventy years before they were able to rebuild Jerusalem's city walls. They did not regain their independence, so were unable to have their own king. For many it seemed as though the exile had not ended: indeed it seems likely that more Jews lived outside the Holy Land than in it from the fall of Jerusalem in 586 BC to time when the Psalter was compiled.

It was in this era, maybe soon after the first return in about 500BC, that the Psalter was put together. Old psalms by David and newer ones were collected together to form the collection we know today. This, however, was not just a random anthology of psalms. It was a carefully organised collection designed to instruct the Jewish believers how to live in their rather discouraging circumstances. Psalms 1 and 2, for example, were deliberately put at the beginning of the collection to encourage the godly to meditate on God's laws enshrined in the psalms and to assure them that they will indeed prosper, if they put God first. For, as Psalm 2 makes plain, God reigns over all the nations through his appointed king in Jerusalem. Therefore, God's people, the Jews, have nothing to fear from their enemies.

That is, at least, what Psalm 2 must have meant when it was first used at royal coronations in Jerusalem. But why put it in such a prominent place in a post-exilic collection when, to the later Jewish readers' distress, there was no Davidic king to save them from their enemies?

This is not the only royal psalm put in such a prominent place in the collection that it sticks out like a sore thumb. The second book of the Psalms closes with Psalm 72, apparently a prayer by David that his son, Solomon, will live while the sun endures (v. 5), and that he will have dominion from sea to sea and that all kings will bow down before him' (vv. 8, 11). Then Book 3 of the Psalter closes with Psalm 89, which ends with the very pointed accusation at God that he has apparently broken his promise to David that he would always have a descendant to rule on his throne.

> 'Once for all, I have sworn by my holiness –
> and I will not lie to David –
> that his line will continue forever
> and his throne endure before me like the sun;
> it will be established forever like the moon,
> the faithful witness in the sky.' *Selah*
> But you have rejected, you have spurned,

you have been very angry with your anointed one.
You have renounced the covenant with your servant
and have defiled his crown in the dust.
(Psalm 89: 35 – 39)

The psalmist cannot believe that this is God's last word. God
does not go back on his promises, so he concludes with a
series of poignant questions.

How long, O LORD? Will you hide yourself forever?
How long will your wrath burn like fire?
(Psalm 89:46)

O Lord, where is your former great love,
which in your faithfulness you swore to David?
(Psalm 89:49)

REFLECTION

- Reflect upon the experience of exile for the Jewish people.
- Think about the crown in the picture at the beginning of this chapter. How might the experience of exile affect the view of God as sovereign King.
- How would you express your prayers in such a situation?
- Think about an individual or a part of the world currently in crisis and turn your thoughts into prayer.

The fourth book of the Psalter represents an answer to these questions. Indeed many recent writers on the psalms argue that this book is the heart of the Psalter. Its theme, expressed most clearly in the opening acclamations of Psalms 93, 97, 99, is that 'the LORD reigns'. Despite appearances, God is king. He is not just Israel's king. He is lord of creation and rules the nations. Implicitly, it compares Israel's situation to her situation in the time of Moses, when the Israelites wandered in the wilderness unable to enter the Promised Land because of their disobedience and unbelief. But the LORD demonstrated his power and his mercy in that era; he may be expected to do so again in the exilic era, if only they 'would hear his voice' and 'not harden your hearts as you did at Meribah, as you did that day at Massah in the desert' (Psalm 95: 7–8).

It is uncertain when these psalms were written. Some definitely appear to have been composed before the exile for the worship in the first temple built by Solomon. Psalms 93–99, which begin 'The LORD reigns' or celebrate his kingship, were most probably written for use then. It is often surmised that God's reign was celebrated in the great autumn festival, the festival of tabernacles.[1] This feast was particularly concerned with Israel's wilderness experiences: it was designed to remind the later Israelites what it was like to live in tents, by making them live in temporary huts called booths or tabernacles (Leviticus 23: 39–43). As we have already noted, the wilderness experiences are often alluded to in this fourth book of the Psalter. Furthermore, in later Jewish worship this season of the year, particularly New Year's day (Rosh Hashanah) was closely associated with

God's kingship. It is, therefore, quite likely that this associa-
tion goes back to the days of the first temple when these
psalms were sung at this time of the year.

On the other hand, some of the psalms in Book 4 definitely seem to have been written with the exilic situation in
mind and should therefore be dated in this period. Psalm
102: 13–16 looks like a clear reference to the exile:

> You will arise and have compassion on Zion,
> for it is time to show favour to her;
> the appointed time has come.
> For her stones are dear to your servants;
> her very dust moves them to pity ...
> For the LORD will rebuild Zion
> and appear in his glory

So does Psalm 106 with its closing prayer: 'Save us O LORD
our God, and gather us from the nations' (v. 47a).

Whether these psalms were originally composed in the
exilic era or much earlier, they are now gathered together to
comment on the situation of the Jews in the exilic period.
All the references to Moses and the wilderness wanderings
are relevant to the Jews in exile, for in both periods they
were outside the Promised Land because of their sins. God's
judgment on Moses and the wilderness generation was in
fact a demonstration of his sovereignty, that he was indeed
king. But paradoxically, God's kingship was, at the same
time, the ground for hope. Israel's exile did not show that
their God had been defeated by the gods of Babylon, but
that their God the LORD was in complete control. This
meant that he could bring them back to the Promised Land,

just as he had brought their forefathers into Canaan centuries before.

Let us quickly glance through the whole of Book 4 before looking at two or three of these psalms more carefully.

Psalm 90 – is entitled 'A Prayer of Moses', the only psalm ascribed to Moses in the Psalter. Its reflections on the transitoriness of life and the power of God are well captured by Isaac Watts' hymn, 'O God our Help in ages past', which is based on this psalm. We shall come back to this psalm again.

Psalm 91 – describes the security of the godly under God's protection.

Psalm 92 – called 'A Song for the Sabbath', is a joyful celebration of God's faithfulness to his people and the defeat of the wicked.

Psalm 93 – the first psalm to begin 'The LORD reigns', affirms God's power over the forces of nature: 'mightier than the waves of the sea, the LORD on high is mighty' (v. 4).

Psalm 94 – strikes a more militant note:

> O LORD, the God who avenges,
> O God who avenges, shine forth.
> Rise up, O Judge of the earth;
> pay back to the proud what they deserve.
> (vv. 1–2)

It goes on to affirm that God will indeed give the proud what they deserve, which greatly reassures the psalmist.

Psalm 95 – is known to Anglicans as the 'Venite', after its opening invitation to '*Come*, let us sing for joy to the LORD'. It invites us to join in joyful worship, but to avoid the mistakes of the wilderness generation, who hardened their hearts and never entered their promised rest (Psalm 95: 8, 11; cf. Hebrews 3:7–18).

Psalm 96 – declares that God is king over all the nations, who should therefore fall down in reverent praise.

Psalm 97 – continues this theme of the LORD's reign: he rules over nature, the nations, his people in Zion, that is Jerusalem, and over all other spiritual powers.

Psalm 98 – invites all creation to sing loud and joyful praise to God, 'for he comes to judge the earth' (v. 9).

Psalm 99 – the final psalm to begin 'The LORD reigns', celebrates the fact that he is a mighty king and lover of justice, but that he also is a forgiving God who answered the prayers of Moses and Aaron, and may be expected to respond to the penitent prayers of later generations too.

Psalm 100 – known to many as the 'Jubilate', or in the metrical version as the Old Hundredth 'All people that on earth do well', is a great summons to praise God for his enduring loving kindness.

Psalm 101 – is one of only two psalms ascribed to David in the fourth book of the Psalter (the other is 103). Here the king defines the sort of civil servant he is looking for.

No one who practices deceit
will dwell in my house;
no one who speaks falsely
will stand in my presence.
(v. 7)

What, commentators ask, is a psalm like this doing in the middle of section celebrating God's kingship? How does it relate to the exilic situation where there was no king? If we see Book 4 of the psalms as a response to the situation in which Israel lost its land and its monarchy, as an answer to the questions of Psalm 89:49, 'Lord, where is thy steadfast love of old, which by thy faithfulness thou didst swear to David?' it is possible to see the inclusion of this psalm as a reaffirmation of faith. Despite Israel's present predicament, God is going to restore a Davidic king and bring the Messiah, but he will require loyal and faithful servants, just as the original David did. In the meantime the LORD is king and he too seeks integrity, loyalty and humility in his servants.

Psalm 102 – this faith in the restoration of Israel's king and land was cruelly tested by the exile. Psalm 102 gives eloquent expression to his despair and yearning that God would return to Zion (vv. 13–17). It is faith in God's kingship that gives the psalmist such confidence: he is eternal and his promises are too (vv. 12, 24–28).

Psalm 103 – in this psalm, joy and confidence break through again as the psalmist remembers that the LORD forgives all your iniquity and heals your diseases (v. 3). This psalm has been turned into that marvellous hymn, 'Praise my soul the King of heaven'.

Psalm 104 – becomes even more lyrical as it praises God as king of creation: the harmonious complementary witness of the whole created order to God's benevolent rule over all his creatures. It ends with the command 'Praise the LORD' or in Hebrew 'Hallelujah', which is used here in the psalms for the very first time, but many more times in subsequent psalms.

Psalm 105 – relates God's dealings with Israel from his covenant with Abraham to the exodus from Egypt and the lawgiving at Sinai, the whole process a demonstration of God's power and faithfulness to his promises. So once again it ends 'Praise the LORD'.

Psalm 106 – the last psalm of Book 4, begins and ends with 'Hallelujah, Praise the LORD'. In its recital of Israel's history the focus is on her disloyalty, not God's loyalty to his promises. Here all the sins of the wilderness period are recalled – the repeated punishment of the Israelites and their frequent cries for help, which were always answered.

> For their sake he remembered his covenant
> and out of his great love he relented.
> (v. 45)

This gives the psalmist confidence to pray:

> Save us, O LORD our God,
> and gather us from the nations,
> that we may give thanks to your holy name

> and glory in your praise.
> (v. 47)

and to end in a doxology[2]

> Praise be to the LORD, the God of Israel,
> from everlasting to everlasting.
> Let all the people say, 'Amen!'
> Praise the LORD.
> (v. 48)

This hasty survey of Book 4 of the Psalter has shown that there are certain themes that are prominent within it: most obviously that the LORD is king despite all appearances. He reigns over nature, the nations and Israel's history. This means that he is in control, even though the nation is mourning its loss of independence and monarchy.

These psalms also draw attention repeatedly to the parallels between Israel's experience in the wilderness and their present experience of exile. Both were caused by their sin, but the LORD is a merciful and forgiving king. Israel's penitence and prayer in the wilderness led to them conquering Canaan centuries earlier: today if they will but listen to his voice they can enjoy restoration again.

REFLECTION

* Pick two Psalms from Psalms 90–106 and read them through carefully.
* Which ideas in these two Psalms are helpful? Which are encouraging and which are challenging?
* Using your chosen Psalms turn them into prayer.

We shall now look at two very different psalms that are found in Book 4 to illustrate these themes in greater detail. We will then address a problem that often troubles readers, the appeals to God to take it out on Israel's foes and punish the wicked.

I have chosen to look at two psalms that are the basis of much loved hymns. The first is Psalm 90, on which Kidner comments: 'Only Isaiah 40 can compare with this psalm for its presentation of God's grandeur and eternity over against the frailty of man.'[3] In reading the psalm we must bear in mind at least two perspectives, that of Moses', to whom the psalm is ascribed and that of the exilic editor of the Psalter, who saw the psalm as having a relevant message for the exiled Israelites.

The psalm divides into two main sections:

(a) Verses 1- 2 reflect on the transitoriness of human life in the light of God's eternity.

(b) Verses 13–17 are petitions for God's mercy despite human sinfulness. The first part forms the basis for the petitions in the second part.

It begins with a reminder of God's long-term concern for his people. 'Lord, you have been our dwelling place throughout all generations'. Moses doubtless was thinking at least as far back as Abraham, centuries before. By the time of the exile another 700 years or more had been added to Israel dwelling under God's protection. What did the recent loss of land and king matter in the light of God's long-term care of his people?

The psalm continues, 700 or 1400 years is as nothing when compared to God's time frame. 'Before the mountains were born or you brought forth the earth and the world, from everlasting to everlasting you are God' (v. 2). It is even less when compared to the human life span:

> The length of our days is seventy years –
> or eighty, if we have the strength;
> yet their span is but trouble and sorrow,
> for they quickly pass, and we fly away.
> (v. 10)

We are well aware of the truth of these lines. News of a local GP's sudden death from a heart attack came just as I was about to comment on these lines. Moses, by the end of his extra long life, had seen most of his contemporaries die in the wilderness, because they had not trusted in God's assurance that they could conquer the Promised Land. Moses knew that he was too destined to die outside the land because of his disobedience. Most of those who went into exile must have died before they returned, and they too realized that their death in exile was the consequence of their sins (cf. Amos 7: 17).

But the psalm generalises much more widely. Not only is the day of our death in God's hands – 'You turn men back to dust, saying, "Return to dust, O sons of men"' (v. 3) – but in a broad sense our days are shortened by our sins:

> You have set our iniquities before you,
> our secret sins in the light of your presence.
> All our days pass away under your wrath ...
> (v. 8)

We are well aware that we can shorten our lives by driving too fast, smoking, drinking or even eating too much, but I think the psalm is making a more general point. We are born into a world of sin; that means every life is lived under the shadow of death. Our only hope is the God who is from everlasting to everlasting. So the psalmist urges: 'Teach us to number our days aright, that we may gain a heart of wisdom' (v. 12).

Commentators debate the meaning of 'numbering our days'. One of them expresses his doubts that it simply means calculating how long it is to retirement and how long we are likely to survive after that. Anyone can surely do that. But as Calvin observes we have a strange reluctance to do it:

> Surely it is a monstrous thing that men should measure all distances within themselves, know how many feet the moon is distant from the centre of the earth, how much space is between planet and planet, and finally to comprehend all the dimensions both of heaven and earth; and yet cannot number threescore and ten years in their own case.[4]

On the other hand, such calculations are not supposed to make us morbid. Rather, as we are told in the book of Ecclesiastes (the book most preoccupied by death in the Bible), we are to rejoice in our life, health, food and youth while we have them. They are gifts from God, which he wants us to enjoy in his fear and favour.

Verse 12, which we have just considered, is a turning point in the psalm. Though it has all been addressed to God, it now becomes a prayer:

Relent, O LORD! How long will it be?
Have compassion on your servants.
Satisfy us in the morning with your unfailing love,
that we may sing for joy and be glad all our days.
Make us glad for as many days as you have afflicted us,
for as many years as we have seen trouble.
May your deeds be shown to your servants,
your splendour to their children.

Here the sentiment of verse 3, 'Return to dust, O sons of men', is taken up and reapplied to God. God tells man to return to dust, but the psalmist now tells God to return to his servants. Such boldness with God in prayer was characteristic of Moses – his prayer was, of course, more than answered. He asked for God to make them glad for as many days as thou hast afflicted us. The Israelites wandered for forty years in the wilderness, but they lived six centuries in Canaan before the Babylonians exiled them. This gives the psalmist great hope that God will act again and save his people. God will continue to ensure a future for his children.

Psalm 90 calls us

to entrust ourselves and our allotted time to God with the assurance that, grounded in God's work and God's time, our lives and labours participate in the eternal. Psalm 90 is finally, therefore, not an act of futility but an act of faith. And it also an act of hope. Without having to see it happen, the psalmist trusts that God can and will satisfy and make glad and make manifest God's work and establish the work of our hands (vv. 14–17).[5]

REFLECTION

- Read and reflect on Psalm 90.
- Read Psalm 90: 12 and Matthew 6: 25–34. How might these verses affect the way we lead our lives?

A PRAYER:

Lord, you are my dwelling place,
From everlasting to everlasting, you are God.
Teach me to number my days aright,
and give me the promised heart of wisdom.
Amen.

Psalm 103, 'Praise my soul the King of heaven' has a totally different feel to it. In Psalm 90, faith is struggling with the transitoriness of life and the frustration of so many of our earthly hopes. In Psalm 103, faith is basking in the sunshine of God's forgiveness. Although the psalm is headed 'a psalm of David', it again looks back to the age of Moses as the period in which God's readiness to forgive was most clearly demonstrated. It quotes, almost word for word, Exodus 34: 6: 'the LORD, the compassionate and gracious God, slow to anger, abounding in love and faithfulness' (cf. Psalm 103: 8). This great declaration was made to Moses immediately after the golden calf incident, when the people had broken the first two commandments and, as a result, God had threatened to destroy the whole people and start afresh with Moses. God, however, relented following Moses' intercession. Indeed, God promised to accompany the Israelites into Canaan and lived among them in the tabernacle. There could have been no clearer demonstration of divine mercy and faithfulness than the outcome of this episode.

The psalm itself divides into three main sections.

In verses 1–5 – the psalmist, David, calls on his whole being to recall all God's blessings to him.

> Praise the LORD, O my soul,
> and forget not all his benefits –
> who forgives all your sins
> and heals all your diseases.

Who better than David could thank God for his mercy in forgiving his sins? He was 'ransomed, healed, restored, forgiven' after committing adultery with Bathsheba and arranging her husband's death.

But this was not a one-off by God. He had acted similarly in Moses' day. The experience of the whole nation in the wilderness period is recalled in the central section of the psalm.

> He made known his ways to Moses,
> his deeds to the people of Israel:
> The LORD is compassionate and gracious,
> slow to anger, abounding in love.
> (vv 7–8)

As we have already noted this is a quotation from the golden calf episode – Israel's most serious sin in the wilderness period. Yet God

> does not treat us as our sins deserve
> or repay us according to our iniquities.
> For as high as the heavens are above the earth,
> so great is his love for those who fear him;
> as far as the east is from the west,
> so far has he removed our transgressions from us.
> (vv. 10–12)

That was most true in the wilderness period. Straight after this episode, God promised that he would accompany the Israelites into Canaan, the tabernacle was built and the cloud of God's glory filled the tabernacle (Exodus 40:34). There could have been no more single demonstration of the greatness of God's forgiveness than this.

What a reassurance to those in exile! They too had sinned greatly; that is why they were outside the land. But if God had forgiven the wilderness generation and dwelt among them in the tabernacle, might the exiles not experience God's grace in similar fashion? Might not the temple be rebuilt and they return to the Promised Land?

The experience of David and Moses shows the constancy of God's character and gives the psalmist great confidence that he will act similarly in future to their descendants.

> But from everlasting to everlasting
> the LORD's love is with those who fear him,
> and his righteousness with their children's children.
> (v. 17)

So in the final part of the psalm, verses 19–20, the psalmist invites all creation to praise the king of heaven. Not just Israel, but all the angels, and all other creatures:

> Angels in the height adore him
> Ye behold him face to face;
> Sun and moon, bow down before him,
> Dwellers all in time and space:
> Alleluia, Alleluia.
> Praise with us the God of grace.

The great theme of this fourth book of the Psalter is God's kingship. He is king of heaven and earth. God is control of all that happens throughout the whole universe. This should prompt us all to join in singing with the heavenly hosts in the words of Handel's Hallelujah chorus, 'King of kings and lord of lords, and he shall reign for ever and ever'. These words taken from Revelation (19:6; 11:15; 19:16) aptly sum up the message of these psalms in Book 4 and the last book of the Bible.

REFLECTION

- Read and reflect on Psalm 103.
- Reflect on what God's forgiveness means to you.
- Read Psalm 103:19 and Revelation 19:6, 11:15 and 19:16. How do you respond to this affirmation of God's kingship over the world?
- Use Psalm 103:20–21 as a prayer.

These psalms and the book of Revelation also contain notes that many modern readers feel uncomfortable with. Often these charming and positive psalms celebrate the fact of God has judged or will judge the wicked. Psalm 96 ends:

> Then all the trees of the forest will sing for joy;
> they will sing before the LORD,
> for he comes, he comes to judge the earth.
> He will judge the world in righteousness
> and the peoples in his truth.
> (vv. 12–13)

Psalm 101 ends:

> Every morning I will put to silence
> all the wicked in the land;
> I will cut off every evildoer
> from the city of the LORD.
> (v. 8)

Even more striking 104, that most tranquil and delightful psalm in praise of God the creator ends:

> But may sinners vanish from the earth
> and the wicked be no more.
> Praise the LORD, O my soul.
> Praise the LORD.
> (v. 35)

Then there is Psalm 94, which begins:

> O LORD, the God who avenges,
> O God who avenges, shine forth.
> Rise up, O Judge of the earth;

pay back to the proud what they deserve.
(v. 1)

It ends:

He will repay them for their sins
and destroy them for their wickedness;
the LORD our God will destroy them.
(v. 23)

How are we to cope with such sentiments? This has long been a problem for Christian readers of the psalms and the commentaries often contain disparaging comments about such imprecations. Throughout Christian history the psalms have been the backbone of worship, and these harsh passages have been in her prayers ever since the Church was formed (e.g. Acts 1:20). In the twentieth century, however, the Church of England lost its nerve. The 1928 prayer book and the ASB (1980) bracket out the more aggressive passages. Though this reduces the problem, it by no means eliminates it, because the picture of God as judge keeps popping up and the psalmists welcome it. Think of Psalm 2 used in the Messiah 'thou wilt smash them in pieces like a potter's vessel', which is placed just before the Hallelujah chorus. Handel's triumphant setting of these phrases expresses the historic Christian celebration of the fact that God reigns and will therefore judge the wicked.

More recently, the same issues have caused controversy among Catholics. Monks and nuns are expected to recite all the psalms in their daily offices. But since Vatican 2, some psalms have been omitted and others abbreviated to remove the offensive passages. This has prompted the most eminent

Catholic commentator on the psalms, who is a monk himself, to write an eloquent defence of this element in the psalms.[6]

Basically, Zenger's book makes two main points. First, all these remarks in the psalms are prayers. They do not express what the psalmists intend to do themselves. They are urgent prayers to God to right the injustice in the world and the wrongs done to his people. They are like the woes that Jesus pronounces on the Pharisees in Matthew 23 or the prayers of the saints in heaven (e.g. Revelation 6: 9–10- 'The souls of those who had been slain because of the word of God … called out in a loud voice, "How long, Sovereign Lord, holy and true, until you judge the inhabitants of the earth and avenge our blood?"').

In our modern world we are more conscious of injustice and violence than at any time in our history. Every TV news programme presents new and appalling cases of violence around the world and on our doorstep. How should we as Christians react to all this? Bury our heads in the sand and say thank goodness it is not happening to me? This is not Zenger's view and I should like to end by including a longish section where is quoting someone else as to why we still need to retain a belief in God's judgement.

> On 8 March 1988, German television presented a film in which the destruction of the little French village of Oradour-sur-Glane was brought to light again. On 10 June 1944, an SS division retaliated against the French Resistance by completely destroying this settlement. In the process, some six hundred men, women and children were burned or shot to death.

One of the officers who commanded this liquidation later lived in the German Democratic Republic as a respected employee in a business establishment, a beloved father and grandfather to his family, attached by the most tender affections to his grandchildren. In 1980, thirty-six years after his deed, he was arrested, prosecuted and sentenced to life imprisonment. A reporter was able to visit him in prison and conducted a long interview with him, during which he wept repeatedly. When the reporter asked, 'Why are you crying now?' he answered, 'Because I have been so happy, and now it ends this way.' The journalist continued, 'Did you ever weep over the children, women, and men you killed that day?' 'No,' he said. 'Did it never occur to you that you had done a terrible injustice to those people?' His answer: 'No, not as long as I was free. Everything was quite normal. But now I often think that there must have been something wrong, that I was involved in it myself somehow, that probably the whole thing was wrong.'

Tears and a slight beginning of remorse, even a hint of recognition of the facts only began for this man when *the judgment of the court* saw to it that he had to face up to the event, so that the deed came back to him, touching him in body and spirit. Now he was in the process of awakening from his obtuse happy captivity in his own well-being and self-satisfaction; now he was beginning to be a human being who sees what he has done. It was judgment that made that possible for him …

The current of our history does not issue in justice, but in the question: Where will it happen? Will it ever appear in its true, comprehensive form? No court, not even the judgment of all humanity, will be adequate to the things that, even now, the people in Bosnia are doing to one another at a distance from us, and others here at home in the intimate circles of their families. What happens in the world of humanity is from its very beginning a cry for God's judgment. And the first response to that cry that is found in the gospel, the *good* news, is:

> The stream of events will not run on forever, over blood and victims, goodness, evil, innocence and justice. *God* will put an end to the course of history and will make clear that there is a difference between justice and injustice, and that this difference must be demonstrated. God will seek out the buried victims, the forgotten, starved children, the dishonoured women, and God will find the hidden doers of these deeds. God will gather all of them before God's eternal, holy will for the good, so that all *must* see how it stands with their lives.[7]

Finally let me read what another great modern commentator, J.L. Mays (an American Presbyterian), has had to say about these psalms:

> Could the use of these prayers remind us and bind us to all those in the world-wide Church who are suffering in faith and for faith? All may be well in our place. There may be no trouble for the present that corresponds to the tribulations described in the Psalms, but do we need to do more than call the roll of such places as El Salvador, South Africa, and China to remember that there are sisters and brothers whose trials could be given voice in our recitation of the Psalms? The old Church believed it was all the martyrs who prayed in their praying the psalmic prayers.

Would it be possible to say them for the sake of and in the name of fellow Christians known to us? We do make intercessions for them, but perhaps these Psalms can help us do more than simply, prayerfully wish grace and help for them, help us to find words to represent their hurt, alienation, failure and discouragement.[8]

I believe first and foremost we should be bringing the needs of suffering Christians around the world to God in our prayers: if you support the Barnabas Fund, for example, you will be aware of the desperate intense suffering of Christians in Moslem countries, such as the Sudan, Pakistan, Indonesia and Nigeria. In many countries, Christians are not just harshly discriminated against; they are murdered or even executed on trumped up charges. We need to pray for them with the same passion that the psalmists showed.

But the need is wider than that: oppression and exploitation of the weak by the strong is endemic in our world. The blood of the victims of the holocausts, Stalin's slave camps, Cambodia, Rwanda, Uganda, Yugoslavia and our very own abortion clinics, should make us pray with all earnestness:

Thy kingdom come, thy will be done, on earth as it is in heaven.
Maranatha, Come Lord Jesus.

REFLECTION

- Look at the picture and think about God as the alpha and the omega, the beginning and the end of world history.
- Consider events of recent history that epitomise evil.
- What do you think of using Psalm 96: 12–13, Psalm 104: 35 and Psalm 94: 23 in our prayer life today?
- How and what should we pray for the tortured and oppressed peoples of the world?
- Reflect upon a world trouble spot and pray for its peoples.

Questions/Activities

1. Try to imagine what it must have felt like to be a Jew living in exile? The fall of Jerusalem was particularly painful for them. What political, social and spiritual reasons made it so painful? What aspects of the modern church's experience or of individual suffering can be compared to the Jews' experience of exile?
2. Which of Psalms 90–106 appeal to you most and why?
3. Read Psalm 90. How much do you reflect on God's eternity and your own mortality? Can you identify with the Psalmist's views? How does the Christian belief in the resurrection change our perspective on these issues?
4. How far do God's past deeds give us encouragement in the present? Share examples from the Bible and more recent times of events and experiences that encourage you.
5. Should we only use the Psalms we are comfortable with in prayer and worship? How ought we to react to oppression and exploitation?

Notes

1. This idea was developed by S. Mowinckel, *The Psalms in Israel's Worship* (Blackwells: Oxford, 1962). He termed them the hymns of Yahweh's enthronement, because at the autumn festival the LORD was ceremonially enthroned as both Israel's king and king of creation. For arguments in favour of their pre-exilic origin, see J. Day, *The Psalms* (Sheffield: Sheffield

Academic Press, 1992) and D. M. Howard, *The Structure of Psalms 93–100* (Winona Lake: Eisenbrauns, 1997).

2. Note how each book of the psalms ends with a doxology. See Psalms 41:13; 72:18,19; 89:52; 106:48; 150:1–6.

3. D. Kidner, *Psalms 73–150* (Leicester: IVP, 1975), 327.

4. J.Calvin, *A Commentary on the Psalms of David II* (London: Thomas Tegg, 1840), 483–84.

5. J.C. McCann Jr, *A Theological Introduction to the Book of the Psalms* (Nashville: Abingdon Press, 1994), 161.

6. E. Zenger, *A God of Vengeance?: Understanding the Psalms of Divine Wrath* (translated by L. M. Maloney. Louisville: Westminster John Knox Press, 1996).

7. G. Bachl, 'Das Gericht', *Christ in der Gegenwart* 45 (1993), 397; quoted in Zenger, *A God of Vengeance*, 67–68.

8. J.L. Mays, 'A Question of Identity: The Three-fold Hermeneutic of Psalmody' (Lecture 2 April 1991) quoted in McCann, *A Theological Introduction to the Psalms*, 117.

The walls have been repaired (cf. the cover) and justice (note the scales) has been finally established. God reigns. This is truly hallelujah territory!

PSALMS 145–150 – 'LET EVERYTHING THAT HAS BREATH ...'

Andrew West

Psalms to read: Psalms 145–150

Praise to the Holiest in the height,
and in the depth be praise;
in all His words most wonderful;
most sure in all His ways.
John Newman

The Psalter begins with blessedness and ends with emphatic praise. In between, it encompasses all the vagaries of our human existence and encapsulates the way of the LORD through instruction and prayer, directing our path in the narrow way. In Psalms 145–150 we encounter the climax of a long journey, the peak of doxology. When we are in the depths, it towers Everest-like above as the promise of something better, the attainment of which refocuses our perspective, creating scale and depth as we survey the landscape that we call 'life'.

This note of praise punctuates the Psalter. We encounter it, for example, in Psalms 8, 100 and 117. We find it splashed as colour in the midst of the blackness of the psalmist's experience. The 'My God, my God, why have you forsaken me' of Psalm 22:1 is countered with 'Yet you are enthroned as the Holy One; you are the praise of Israel' in verse 3. In Psalm 73 it is in the sanctuary (v. 17) that the psalmist perceives the perspective needed to comprehend the injustice that torments the soul. Admittedly, for most of the time, life is not black, but even predictable magnolia can benefit from the dash of colourful variety which praise can generate. Praise should punctuate our experiences of daily living and in some way transcend the pain, numbness or even plain ordinariness of our existence.

The Psalter is like a theological journey, which reaches its climax in the shout of 'hallelujah'. Part of its message to the people of God (at times living in exile) is that lament and complaint is not the end of the road. Books 1–3 are characterized by cries of lament and complaint, but praise asserts itself in Books 4–5.[1] The Psalter is structured theologically; it moves successively from lament to praise and culminates in the lavish doxology of Psalms 145–150. It presents a picture of life, which is fulfilled in the activity of declaring the praises of the sovereign lord, Yahweh. For Christians, this movement evokes memories of a journey specific to Jesus, and yet paradigmatic of our experience of life; that from cross to resurrection.

So let us conclude this exploration of the Psalter by considering each of these psalms individually and from them constructing a map of praise to plot our path through the landscape of our lives.

1. A Journey of Praise

Step One Psalm 145 – an all-encompassing praise

(a) The *daily* and *eternal* characteristics of praise (vv. 1–2), which we encounter in this psalm, display the vast scope of doxology. Praise is offered in the reality of our time-and-space universe, but it also transcends it in the timelessness of God. Praise is built into the fabric of everyday living, which has the potential for eternity. It is offered in the here and now (e.g. on the hospital ward, on the factory production line, in the daily chores of home-making or in the library poring over the minutiae of medieval history) and it is also caught up in the flow of ceaseless praise offered eternally before the throne of Almighty God.

Praise is also *individual* and *corporate*: 'I will exalt you my God the King' (v. 1); 'they will speak of the glorious splendour of your majesty' (v. 5). In verses 5–6 we can see these two come together – the first line of each verse speaks of the community in worship and the second line of the individual (this is clear in the Hebrew but not in all English translations). It is interesting to note the themes of proclamation and meditation also present in these verses. Individually and corporately God's people proclaim the greatness of God and are called to ponder and reflect on the significance of God's actions in history. Thus praise is not an irrational activity, it requires thought and it is rooted in the reality of God's creative and redemptive involvement in his world.

(b) We also encounter two truths about Yahweh, which should stimulate our praise, in this psalm.

Praise is offered to the *God who has acted in history through his mighty works* (vv. 3–7). Within the Psalter as a whole Israel looks back in the psalms of worship and of lament to the saving power of the LORD displayed on many occasions – particularly such formative moments in the history of Israel as the crossing of the Red Sea, the law-giving at Sinai and the conquest of the land. The people's praise of Yahweh is rooted in his saving activity in history on behalf of his people.

Praise is also offered in *response to the character of God* (vv. 8–20): Yahweh is compassionate, faithful and righteous. He is sovereign over all creation with a concern for the burdened and the hungry. Tom Wright reminds us that Yahweh is not 'just the tribal God of Israel, but the God of all the earth, the healing, liberating God, the God of creation and covenant, of Exodus, wilderness and Jordan, the God of steadfast redeeming love.'[2] The people of God are to offer an all-encompassing praise to an all-encompassing God.

Verse 8 is a quote from Exodus 34:6 already encountered in relation to Psalm 103:8. This quote from Exodus recurs in the pages of the Old Testament. It is an important reminder of the nature of God. As a revelation of God's character it moulds the experience and hopes of his people. In the context of these praises it is foundational in understanding the nature of the LORD, the one who is worshipped. It speaks of his mercy but not of a cheap grace. It is a statement of the character of God in the midst of judgement following the sin of Israel in making the golden calf. It is a facet of God's nature to reach out and bestow undeserved compassion and mercy, which motivates our adoration. Hardy and Ford put it like this 'Praise is … an attempt to cope with the abundance of God's love.'[3]

(c) The structure of Psalm 145 affirms the *comprehensiveness of praise*. This psalm is the last acrostic psalm in the Psalter. The content and the alphabetic structure of the psalm reinforce the message and create a portrait of praise that is both endless and complete.

REFLECTION

- List the things that most concern you in your life at present.
- Reflect on whether they stimulate you to praise or to lament/complaint.
- Trace the love and mercy of God throughout your life.

A PRAYER:

My Lord is gracious and compassionate,
Slow to anger and rich in love.
My Lord is good to all, He has compassion on all he has made.
My Lord was despised and rejected, sorrowful and suffering, He
was pierced for sin, crushed and punished:
But by His wounds we are healed.
Hallelujah! Amen.

Step Two Psalm 146 – encountering the purpose of praise

The remainder of these Psalms all begin and end with the same Hebrew word hallelujah, in English a call to 'praise the LORD'. This call of hallelujah embraces these psalms just as praise should embrace the life of the believer and the believing community.

In this hymn we engage with the kingship of Yahweh, which is the foundation of praise, trust and faith. The LORD is contrasted with the 'princes … who cannot save' (v. 3); they are mortal and last but a lifetime (v. 4). Yahweh, however, is 'the maker of heaven and earth' (v. 6) and the faithful one.

In verses 7–9 we encounter Yahweh on the side of the marginalized. He supports the oppressed, feeds the hungry, sets the captives free, opens the eyes of the blind, lifts up the burdened and watches over the alien, the orphan and the widow. All too often humankind in need looks to political leaders, as in verse 3, to plead their case and change their plight, but in vain. Only Yahweh can help because 'the LORD reigns for ever' (v. 10).

In the picture at the front of this chapter the crown is represented above the praises of the psalms, Yahweh reigns and hence we praise.

It is in this certain reign of God that we encounter the true purpose of doxology. Praise is an acknowledgement of the greatness of the creator, redeemer, sustainer God who acts in history to save a people for himself and pleads their cause. Hardy and Ford remind us that at the centre of the Jewish and Christian tradition is the idea of taking 'up the whole of life into praises of God, making him central to everything and his glory the goal of the universe.'[4]

For the Christian these verses are evocative of the story of Jesus Christ, which will later become *the* story of God's dealing with his world. In Matthew 11:1–6, John the Baptist, whilst in prison, sends his disciples to question Jesus. He receives an answer that reveals Jesus to be the one who delivers the fullness of salvation spoken of in verses 7–8 of this psalm. In the Nazareth synagogue Jesus declares himself to be the one who fulfils the prophecy of Isaiah 61.[5] These accounts teach us that God in Christ is on our side meeting our deepest needs. This is good news! The people of God are called to witness to this good news with lives that respond to the needs of, for example, the imprisoned Burmese democrat, the starving child in Ethiopia and the Gulf War veteran reduced to hostel living in the midst of a soulless city, in the hope that they can encounter the purposes of God for his world and enter the excitement of declaring his praises.

It is this assurance of God's presence with us that forms the last beatitude of the Psalter (v. 5). Those who are 'approved by God' are those who know in all its fullness the help and hope of Yahweh as they trust in his sovereign rule.

REFLECTION

- List the things that most concern you about the wider world at present.
- Reflect on whether these world events stimulate you to praise or to lament/praise.
- In the picture at the beginning of this chapter what do you think is the significance of the crown above the scroll?
- What does it mean to say 'The Lord reigns for ever' (Psalm 146 v10) in these circumstances?

A PRAYER:

> *Praise the Lord!*
> *Who upholds the cause of the oppressed,*
> *Who lifts up those bowed down,*
> *Who sustains the fatherless and the widow.*
> *Praise the Lord!*
> *Who gave sight to the blind and made the lame walk,*
> *Who made the deaf to hear and preached good news to the poor.*
> *Lord who reigns forever, reign in me, reign in your world.*
> *For Christ's sake. Amen.*

Step three Psalm 147 – praising and learning

Psalm 1 introduces us to the Psalter as a book concerned with torah, God's instruction of his people. In Psalm 147 we are presented with reflections of God's attributes, in the context of praise, which instruct us in the truth about him. Mays comments 'The Lord is so much the content of praise that praise begins to reflect his attributes.'[6] It is a consequence of singing the praises of Yahweh that we learn more of him and experience more of his goodness (v. 1).

We learn that the God we praise is the saviour (vv. 2–6). He meets the needs of his chosen people, ending their exile and restoring Jerusalem (vv. 2–3). However this is no mere national deity. His concern is also universal for he 'determines the number of the stars' (v4). We praise a God who concerns himself with the particular and the universal. This is Yahweh who grants peace to Israel (v. 14) and controls the climate (vv. 15–17). His creating and sustaining of the world is allied to his choosing and protecting of his people. It is the same God who does both. It is Yahweh who called Abraham and promised through his descendants to bless all the peoples of the world (Genesis 12) and who, through the cross of Christ, is creating peace and reconciliation in his creation for the totality of heaven and earth (Colossians 1:20). This wonderful God includes in his purpose of salvation for his people a plan for the restoration and liberty of the whole created order (Romans 8:19–21). Thus the God who sustains the world and acts in the natural order, causing grass to grow and clouds to roam the skies (v. 8) is the same God who revealed his word to Jacob, his Torah to Israel

(v. 19). We sense here echoes of Psalm 19 where creation and word come together in the creative and revelatory nature of God.

Psalm 147, therefore, calls us to praise, to shout hallelujah, and then instructs us about the one we praise. Our God is the God of the universal and the particular. This truth about God demands our praise and worship but our praise and worship should nourish in us this truth about God.

Step four Psalm 148 – entering the unity of praise

> From the beginning you have created all things
> and all your works echo the silent music of your praise.[7]

In this Psalm the praise offered to God is in the heavens verses 1–6 and on the earth verses 8–14 and it is pictured as being offered by nature and by humankind. We are brought face to face with a completed week of praise as every creation day of Genesis 1 is linked in adoration of its maker.

The hallelujah is to sound in the heavens from the angels and in the skies from the stars. Yahweh set by divine decree their place in the order of created reality and the psalmist, in technicolour imagery, urges on them a response of unadulterated adoration. Thus the cosmos expresses its dependence on the creator in hymns of continual praise (vv. 5–6).

In verses 7–10 the scene changes to the surface of the earth. The natural world of fauna, flora, landscape and the extremes of weather are pictured as being enveloped in this mounting splendour of doxology, a unity of adoration. The sentence summoning the earth to praise that began in verse

7 continues into verses 11–12 as the picture shifts to human-kind. The all-embracing call includes the entire human race from monarchs to children. Our modern world knows these distinctions too. World leaders luxuriate at state banquets and the children of the poor drink dirty water, or worse have no water at all. Yet praise is a great leveller. For the praises of all are of equal worth to God in his kingdom where the first shall be last and the last first.

Verse 14 deserves closer attention. Psalm 148 has presented us with a symphony of praise that encompasses all creation. The psalmist tells us in verse 6 that this is in response to God's act of creation. However, for the people of Israel then, and the people of God today there is another reason for entering this cosmic hymn of praise: redemption. In v14 we read of the 'horn'. This is an image of God's gift of blessing and in the New Testament is wonderfully revealed in a hymn of praise by Zechariah: 'He has raised up a horn of salvation for us in the house of his servant David' (Luke 1:69)

God's promise to David of a kingship perpetually secure in his line of descent, of which we are reminded in Psalms 90–106, is here fulfilled in Jesus. Israel was called to praise her saviour God the bestower of blessing. Christians praise the same Yahweh who in Jesus has raised up a horn of blessing and favour unsurpassable. Our response can only be that of 'hallelujah'!

REFLECTION

- List the ways in which you enjoy God's creation.
- Consider how you have experienced God's salvation.
- Turn your thoughts into prayer and praise of your creator and redeemer God, who is Father, Son and Holy Spirit.

Step five Psalm 149 – praise and politics

> Not for the lip of praise alone,
> nor e'en the praising heart,
> I ask, but for a life made up
> of praise in every part.
> Horatius Bonar

Psalm 149 begins with the now familiar call to 'praise the LORD' which is pictured in the context of corporate worship, 'the assembly of the saints' (v. 1). Movement through verses 2–5 reinforces this with references to music and dancing. The call to 'Israel' and the 'people of Zion' place this praise in the context of covenant. In these verses, therefore, we inhabit the realm of nationhood and kingship, of Jerusalem and temple. These are the symbols that define God's promises to his Old Testament people and the historical realities they forfeited in the period of the exile. Praise proceeds from real life, including the civil and the political.

This is reinforced in verses 6–9. With praise in her mouth Israel has a responsibility to execute the judgement of God on the nations, carrying a two-edged sword in her hand. In Psalm 2 we encountered the image of a league of nations united against the anointed one of Yahweh. In Psalm 149 a praising people of God are dispatched as the bearers of divine judgement against all that is in opposition to the gentle rule of God (it is the scales of justice, evenly balanced, which are pictured in the centre of our praise in the picture for this chapter). Those who praise God in daily and sabbath worship in the hymns of the psalms must also praise God in the world, embodying and struggling for his righteousness amidst rebellion and oppression.

Christian people throughout the ages have lived and continue to live in the shadow of the cross. At Calvary, the cosmic forces of evil and the political and religious powers of the day nailed Jesus to the cross. On that same cross, the vengeance and justice of God was at work reordering history to defeat the forces of death and evil in resurrection power. A new people of praise emerged in the flow of that victory. A people sent into the world armed with the truth of Christ, the sword which is 'sharper than any two-edged sword' and which judges the 'thoughts and attitudes of the heart' (Hebrews 4:12); a praising people who hear and respond to the call of Christ to 'seek first his kingdom and his righteousness' (Matthew 6:33). In this act of seeking, such a people reveal the judgement of God who longs to reorder lives, communities, nations and the world in line with his righteousness and rule and for his praise and glory. How to do this in the service of the Prince of Peace demands thought. It is not to be in the dress of crusaders with a literal sword whatever our history reveals. Rather, it is to be like that solitary student captured on our television screens who stood alone against the terror of dictatorial power in the face of a Chinese tank in Tiananmen Square. It is to daily 'pick up our cross' and follow Jesus.

REFLECTION

- Consider the scales of justice in the middle of the scroll of praise in the picture for this chapter.
- List some of the people, places and organisations in which you are involved.
- Reflect on how you can serve (live a life of praise) in these situations to further the righteousness of God.
- Pray for these people/situations seeking God's holy will for them.

Step six Psalm 150 – a crescendo of praise

The last word is praise, praise for praise's sake. As Brueggemann says 'Psalm 150 is remarkable because it contains no reason or motivation at all.'[8] All these Psalms begin with an imperative to praise. Psalm 150 remains there throughout until we arrive at the final verse (v. 6).

- *We are told who we should praise* – the sovereign Lord God and King, revealed as Yahweh to his people Israel (v. 1).
- *We are told where this act of praising takes place* – in the sanctuary and in the heavens (v. 1), a reminder to us of Psalm 148.
- *We are told why we praise Yahweh* – for his acts of power and his inherent greatness (v. 2), a summary of Psalms 145 and 147.
- *We are told how to praise our God* – with a lengthy list of musical instruments and with dance. This is joyful and loud praise (vv. 3–5). We are here reminded that the Psalter is a hymnbook and that references to musical instructions litter the book.
- *We are told who should praise* – all creatures with breath in their bodies are to shout 'hallelujah'!

Praise is offered at the conclusion of the Psalter by those who have prayed and sung the Psalms as the songs of their corporate history and of their personal lives. Those who have been betrayed by friends and those whose experience is seemingly akin to being forsaken by God and crushed by enemies praise God. These are the hymns of those frustrated at the success of the evil ones and by the dishonouring of the

LORD. These are the songs of the people of Yahweh who have looked back and recorded in their worship the actions of God in history, in creation and in saving a people for himself. All who have had these experiences in their lives are, in Psalm 150, captured in life-transforming, ecstatic praise of the LORD.

Psalms 145–150 conclude the Psalter and Psalm 150 concludes the final part of the Psalter and incorporates all that has gone before.

The Final Step – 'Let everything that has breath praise the LORD'

In the context of praising God the final step is not a finale but a beginning. Praise allows us metaphorically to soar above our world and to change the focus of our vision. We need this experience to help liberate us from the Western, consumerist society, which directs us in the paths of mammon and places 'I' at the centre. We inhabit a world that values and promotes the pampering of the self. Praise serves to challenge this self-centredness and to relativize the individualism that drives the juggernaut of modern life.

Speaking of the Psalms Brueggemann says:

> These songs portray Israel's readiness to cede itself over to God, and its readiness to abandon itself in gratitude and amazement to God. Israel sings of the one who is in the midst of the world in fidelity and generosity, and who is resolved to remain faithful until all is well in the coming age. Such doxological affirmation is a profound act of

devotion to God, but also an act of resistance, a refusal to give in to the deathly reality of circumstance.[9]

For ultimately praise is about the other, and the other has a name:

Yahweh,

and

Jesus Christ, in whom the fullness of Yahweh was pleased to dwell (Colossians 2:9).

In doxology we lose ourselves in the acknowledgement of the glory of God. We are lifted from the pain and the drudgery of this life, from the second-best, into a world of awe. We join our praises with the heavens, the skies and all God's creation. We enter a world touched and changed by grace and mercy. Here with Horatius Bonar we are driven to plead

Fill Thou my life, O Lord my God,
in every part with praise,
that my whole being may proclaim
Thy being and Thy ways.

At the conclusion of this journey of praise the last words must belong to the Psalmist:

'Let everything that has breath praise the LORD.'

REFLECTION

- What have you learnt about praise from these Psalms?
- How can you develop praise in your prayers, worship and life?

A PRAYER:

> *Almighty God,*
> *Your Son has opened for us*
> *a new and living way into your presence.*
> *Give us pure hearts and steadfast wills*
> *To worship you in spirit and in truth;*
> *Through the same Jesus Christ our Lord.*
> *Amen.*[10]

Questions/Activities

Read Psalms 8, 100, 117 and 145–150

1. Having read these Psalms, share together from them, what has encouraged, excited or challenged you about 'praise'.

2. Select a news event from the past week. Reflect on how God is King in his world. Discuss how the Psalms enabled praise to happen in a broken world. Consider how praise can be part of our response to contemporary 'news'.

3. Consider how you spend your week. Discuss how our daily lives can reflect our call to be a praising people. In Psalm 149 praising people are encouraged to pronounce God's judgement in the world. How might Christians today do that, by word and deed, in their places of work, leisure and homes?

4. Consider how praise is expressed in the worship of your church. Share together how you think this can be developed in light of these Psalms.

5. The people of Israel were led to praise Yahweh for his actions in saving them. Read and meditate on one or more of the following Bible passages considering what God in Christ has done for our salvation, share together your thoughts and turn them into praise.

   John 1:1–18
   Luke 23:26 – 24:12
   Acts 2:1–13
   Luke 16:11–32

Notes

1. J. Clinton McCann Jr, *A Theological Introduction to the Psalms* (Nashville: Abingdon Press, 1993), 53, and Patrick Miller, *Interpreting the Psalms* (Philadelphia: Fortress Press, 1986), 67.

2. Tom Wright, *The Way of the Lord* (London: Triangle SPCK, 1999), 28.

3. D.W. Hardy and D.F. Ford, *Jubilate: Theology in Praise* (London: Darton Longman and Todd, 1984), 1

4. Ibid., 8.

5. Lk. 4:14–21.

6. J.L. Mays, *Psalms* (Louisville: John Knox Press, 1994), 442.

7. Church Of England, *Common Worship* (London: Church House Publishing, 2000), 201.

8. Walter Brueggemann, *The Psalms and the Life of Faith* (Minneapolis: Fortress Press, 1995), 192.

9. Walter Brueggemann, 'A Journey: Attending to the Abyss' in *Transmission* Spring (2000), 7.

10. Church of England, *Alternative Service Book* (Cambridge: CUP, Colchester: Wm Clowes and London: SPCK, 1980), Collect for Pentecost 20, 733–734

The crown of thorns that forms a cross with the staff depicts the fact that the suffering of Christ is central to the New Testament. The four segments contain the traditional symbols of the Gospels: Matthew = the angel, Mark = the lion, Luke = the ox, John = the eagle. Open books now replace the scrolls in the previous pictures; God's plan for salvation has been revealed in Christ.

6

Proclaiming the Reign of Christ, the Lord

The Psalms in the New Testament

Karl Möller

Psalms to read: Psalms 2, 22, 69, 110, 118.

No other Old Testament book is quoted or referred to more often in the New Testament than the book of Psalms. While in Judaism the Torah was, and still is, at the centre of the worship and life of the believer, in the early church the prophetic writings and the psalms had taken on a prominent role. To everyone taking the time to look into the use of the psalms in the New Testament, it will soon become clear that the Psalter was of great importance, as the first Christians sought to understand, proclaim, explain and defend that Jesus Christ was indeed the long-awaited Messiah. In particular, his followers had come to believe that, through his death and resurrection, he had established the reign of the LORD that the Psalms both affirmed and anticipated.

The New Testament writers were obviously very familiar with Israel's ancient songs and prayers; this is illustrated not least by the large number of quotations taken from many different psalms. Yet time and again they kept coming back to Psalms such as 2, 22, 69, 110 and 118, because they were found to be particularly illuminating for telling and understanding the teaching and ministry of Christ. However, before we go on to look at the use of the psalms in the New Testament, we need to ask why they were of such great importance to the first Christians.

Clinton McCann has given a brief but apt answer to this question. He points out that the 'theological heart' of the book of Psalms is basically the same as Jesus' proclamation that the LORD reigns.[1] While Jesus announces the actual arrival of the kingdom of God, the psalmists, many centuries earlier, asserted the same fundamental conviction – it is the LORD who rules in all the earth. It is no wonder, then, that those who penned the books of the New Testament made heavy use of the psalms in their portrayal of and reflection on the one who they believed these ancient texts ultimately were all about (cf. Luke 24:44).

But it is worth looking a little closer to find out what exactly the first Christians made of the psalms and, in particular, how and in what ways they related them to their Lord, the crucified and risen Christ.

1. How Did the New Testament Writers Read the Psalms?

In the New Testament the psalms are read, interpreted and used in at least three different ways. First, the Gospel accounts of the passion of Jesus illustrate the profound influence these texts have had on the thinking and the prayer life of our Lord. Secondly, for those who had come to believe in Jesus as the Son of God, the psalmists' references to Yahweh, their rock, fortress, shepherd, way, truth and life, became applicable also to the Messiah, who had at last established God's kingdom on earth. Finally, and perhaps most importantly, the first Christians had come to read the psalms in a completely new light, having become convinced of their prophetic role in forecasting the kingship of the suffering Christ.[2]

The Psalms Are the Prayers of Christ

The passion narratives in particular abound with passages in which Christ is seen making the language and the images of the psalms his own. The first example comes from the Last Supper. It was customary for those sharing in the Passover meal to conclude the table fellowship by singing some of the 'Hallel' psalms (Psalms 113–118), which is precisely what Jesus and the disciples seem to have done before they set out for Gethsemane (cf. Matthew 26:30; Mark 14:26). Later on, when they had entered the garden, Jesus asked his disciples to keep him company saying that his soul was 'overwhelmed with sorrow to the point of death' (Matthew

26:38; Mark 14:34). These words (which appear to be an allusion to Psalms 42:3, 5–6, 11; 43:5) indicate how Jesus expressed his fear and anxiety in the language of the Psalter.

But the great influence of the psalms on his thinking and praying is nowhere more obvious than at the crucifixion when, as the Gospel writers concur in telling us, Jesus keeps quoting Israel's ancient prayers. Most famous are the cry of abandonment, 'My God, my God, why have you forsaken me?' (Matthew 27:46; Mark 15:34; cf. Psalm 22:1), and the word of commitment, 'Father, into your hands I commit my spirit' (Luke 23:46; cf. Psalm 31:5).

There may be a further allusion to the Psalms in the words 'I am thirsty' in John 19:28. Inconspicuous though they sound, John is adamant that Jesus said them deliberately so that the Scriptures would be fulfilled. In this case, it is not entirely clear precisely which passage Jesus, or John, had in mind. They could have been alluding to Psalm 22:15, where the words 'my tongue sticks to the roof of my mouth' form one of the many body metaphors used to describe the psalmist's desperate condition. Alternatively, Jesus may have been referring to his spiritual thirst for God, in which case the allusion could have been to a phrase like 'my soul thirsts for you' in Psalm 63:1.

Dietrich Bonhoeffer, taking his cue from passages such as these, emphasized that the psalms in general – not just the odd one or two of them – are the prayers of Christ. As he put it, 'in the Psalms of David the promised Christ himself already speaks'.[3] Bonhoeffer in particular referred to Hebrews 2:12 and 10:5, two verses in which the anonymous author of Hebrews quotes from Psalms 22:22 and 40:6–8, stressing that these are the words of Christ. Thus, in the Psalms

> it is the incarnate Son of God, who has borne every human weakness in his own flesh, who here pours out the heart of all humanity before God and who stands in our place and prays for us. He has known torment and pain, guilt and death more deeply than we. Therefore it is the prayer of the human nature assumed by him which comes here before God. It is really our prayer, but since he knows us better than we know ourselves and since he himself was true man for our sakes, it is also really his prayer …[4]

The Psalms Can Now Be Prayed to Christ, the Son of God

Whereas in Old Testament times these ancient songs and prayers were addressed to Yahweh, the God of Israel, the first Christians continued to use the psalmists' images that speak of Yahweh's protection, sustenance and guidance but applied them to Jesus Christ, the Son of God.

To give only one example, the Psalms and the New Testament frequently use water imagery in order to express two rather different ideas.[5] Thus, while the psalms abound with references to the life-sustaining and refreshing quality of fresh or living water, there are also numerous passages that emphasize the life-threatening power of the so-called 'chaos waters'. An illustration of the former concept can be found in Psalm 42:1–2, where we find the well-known words,

> As the deer pants for streams of water,
> so my soul pants for you, O God.
> My soul thirsts for God, for the living God.

By contrast, the following passage exemplifies the negative, dangerous side of water as an anti-godly force, which is, however, kept under control by Yahweh:

> O LORD God Almighty, who is like you?
> You are mighty, O LORD, and your faithfulness surrounds you.
> You rule over the surging sea; when its waves mount up, you
> still them.
> (Psalm 89:8–9)

The writer of Psalms 42–43 looks to Yahweh as the source that will quench his thirst. In the New Testament, however, the source has changed in that the Gospel of John now portrays Jesus as the living water, and invites those who are thirsty to come to *him* instead (John 4:13–15; 7:37–38). Similarly, while the psalms celebrate the God of Israel as the one who keeps the threatening forces of the waters in check, the first Christians believed in the Son of God who rebuked the wind and commanded the waves to be quiet (Mark 4:35–41). No wonder Jesus' disciples 'were terrified and asked each other, "Who is this? Even the wind and the waves obey him!"' (Mark 4:41).

REFLECTION

- What role do the Psalms play in our own spiritual lives?
- What can we learn from Jesus' use of the Psalms in his prayers?
- How can we use the Psalms in our own prayer lives?
- Use a Psalm that speaks into your current situation as a prayer.

The Psalms Are Prophecies about Christ

It is the Psalter – not the book of Isaiah, as one might think, – that is used more often than any other Old Testament book for a prophetic purpose.[6] A good illustration of this prophetic use of the psalms is Peter's speech at Pentecost. In it, he sets out to demonstrate that the strange events involving the one whom Christians had come to believe to be the Christ – which the Jews found rather difficult to swallow – had already been foretold in the Scriptures. In his attempt to convince the Jews that Jesus was indeed the expected Messiah, Peter quotes from a number of Old Testament passages, including the following one from Psalm 16:8–11:

> I saw the Lord always before me.
> Because he is at my right hand, I will not be shaken.
> Therefore my heart is glad and my tongue rejoices;
> my body also will live in hope,
> *because you will not abandon me to the grave,*
> *nor will you let your Holy One see decay.*
> You have made known to me the paths of life;
> you will fill me with joy in your presence.
> (Acts 2:25–28; cf. Psalm 16:8–11)

These, as Peter points out, are David's words (cf. Acts 2:25). However, as there cannot be any doubt that David did die and see decay (v. 29), he could not have been speaking about himself. Instead, Peter concludes, in prophetic fashion he saw 'what was ahead' and 'spoke of the resurrection of the Christ, that *he* was not abandoned to the grave, nor did *his* body see decay' (v. 31).

But it is not only the apostles who read the Psalms in the light of Jesus' ministry. As Luke informs us, they only continued a practice they had learned from their master, who himself had taught them that, ultimately, Israel's songs and prayers were about none other than the Christ (Luke 24:44). Thus, for instance, at the Last Supper Jesus justified his choice of disciples, including the one who was to betray him, by pointing out that, instead of having made a mistake, his choice of Judas Iscariot had been a deliberate one. In what he had done, he had been concerned to make sure that the Scriptures would be fulfilled, which had forecast that 'he who shares my bread has lifted up his heel against me' (John 13:18; cf. Psalm 41:9).

As the prophetic interpretation of the psalms is arguably the angle that was of most importance to the New Testament writers, we will have to look at this in more detail. However, before we do so, it needs to be said that the prophetic understanding of these ancient poems is not something the Christians, or indeed Jesus, had suddenly come up with themselves. Far from it; they all were practising a type of interpretation that was common currency in first-century Judaism. For instance, the texts discovered in a number of caves near Qumran at the Dead Sea reveal to us a community that regarded many of the psalms, as well as other Old Testament passages, as prophecies that could be applied directly to their own situation.

One example must suffice at this point. In Psalm 37:21–22 we read:

> The wicked borrow and do not repay,
> but the righteous give generously;
> those the LORD blesses will inherit the land,
> but those he curses will be cut off.

The Qumran community read these verses as a prophecy applying to their own situation, as is shown by the following explanation:

> Interpreted, this concerns the congregation of the Poor, who [shall possess] the whole world as an inheritance. They shall possess the High Mountain of Israel [for ever], and shall enjoy [everlasting] delights in His Sanctuary. [But those who] shall be cut off, they are the violent [of the nations and] the wicked of Israel; they shall be cut off and blotted out for ever.
> (from 4Q171)[7]

Thus, according to this interpretation, Psalm 37:21–22 is not just about the righteous in general, it is about the 'congregation of the Poor', i.e. the community of Qumran. They will gain dominance over Israel while the 'wicked of Israel', i.e. those outside the Qumran sect, will be 'blotted out for ever'.

But what gave rise to these prophetic interpretations? As far as the psalms are concerned, there is reason to conclude that the prophetic readings are not an arbitrary way of understanding them, but that they have been triggered by the Psalter itself. In particular, many of the so-called 'royal psalms', which in their original Old Testament setting focus on the Israelite king, have a dimension that all but calls for a Messianic reading. Psalm 2, for instance, envisages that the king of Israel will rule over the nations and will possess the 'ends of the earth' (Psalm 2:8–9). Psalm 72, too, paints a picture of an ideal king:

> He will judge your people in righteousness,
> your afflicted ones with justice.
>
> He will defend the afflicted among the people
> and save the children of the needy;
> he will crush the oppressor.
> He will endure as long as the sun,
> as long as the moon, through all generations.
> He will be like rain falling on a mown field,
> like showers watering the earth.
> In his days the righteous will flourish;
> prosperity will abound till the moon is no more.
> He will rule from sea to sea
> and from the River to the ends of the earth.
>
> All kings will bow down to him
> and all nations will serve him.
> For he will deliver the needy who cry out,
> the afflicted who have no one to help.
> He will take pity on the weak and the needy
> and save the needy from death.
> He will rescue them from oppression and violence,
> for precious is their blood in his sight.
> (Psalm 72:2, 4–8, 11–14)

It goes without saying that no Israelite king ever lived up to these ideals and so the Jews began to look to the expected Messiah as the one who would eventually fulfil these words.

And this, the New Testament writers claim, is what has happened in Jesus: *he* is the king whose reign is marked by peace,
justice and righteousness and whose kingdom is universal,
encompassing all the earth.

REFLECTION

- How does the picture at the beginning of this chapter relate to the prophetic interpretation of the Psalms by the New Testament writers?
- What does it express about the relationship between the psalms and the life and ministry of Jesus?
- Use the Lord's Prayer as a way of praying for God's kingdom to come.

2. The Psalms and the Christ

Telling the Story of Jesus: The Psalms in the Gospels

Clinton McCann has helpfully shown how, time and again, the Psalms are brought into play at crucial points in the story of Jesus' earthly life and ministry.[8] It starts at Jesus' birth when, as Luke informs us, the heavenly host praise God saying,

> Glory to God in the highest,
> and on earth peace to men on whom his favour rests.
> (Luke 2:14)

McCann is right, I believe, to suggest that these words are reminiscent of Psalm 29 (cf. esp. vv. 1–2, 9), an enthronement psalm that celebrates and proclaims Yahweh's rule as king. The point in Luke 2, then, appears to be that God, in a sense, is now being enthroned in the birth of Jesus, whose arrival ushers in the kingdom of God.

When later on, at the baptism, a heavenly voice says, 'You are my Son, whom I love' (Mark 1:11; cf. also Matthew 3:17; Luke 3:22), we are again reminded of the psalms. This time, the quote is from Psalm 2:7 where God installs his king, 'his Anointed One' (Psalm 2:2), addressing him with these words. The Gospel writers use the reference to emphasize that, right at the outset of Jesus' ministry, he is the Davidic king, the Messiah the Jews had been waiting for for such a long time. This is reaffirmed some time later at the transfiguration when a cloud envelops Jesus and the disciples and a voice from the cloud quotes the same passage to remind the disciples that Jesus is indeed God's chosen Son (Matthew 17:5; Mark 9:7; Luke 9:35).

Craig Bartholomew, in his chapter on Psalms 1 and 2, stressed the links of the first two psalms with the beatitudes in Matthew 5:1–12. According to Matthew, Jesus began his teaching ministry with a series of blessings, just as the book of Psalms starts by blessing the one who delights in the instruction of the LORD (Psalm 1:2) and takes 'refuge in him' (Psalm 2:12). When Jesus, in the third beatitude, promises the meek that *they* 'will inherit the earth' (Matthew 5:5), he is in fact renewing an old promise already made in Psalm 37:11. While our experience tells us that the wicked 'bring down the poor and needy' (Psalm 37:14), both Jesus and the psalmist of old affirm that it is the meek who will eventually prevail over them – for the 'power of the wicked will be broken' (v. 17) and they will finally perish (v. 20).

Another event in the ministry of Jesus that is interpreted in the light of the psalms is the cleansing of the temple. This time it is John who tells us that Jesus' actions, when he overturned the tables of the money changers and drove them all out of the temple, reminded the disciples of the words in Psalm 69:9, 'for zeal for your house consumes me' (John 2:17).

According to the synoptic Gospels, the cleansing of the temple was preceded by Jesus' triumphant entry into Jerusalem (Matthew 21:1–11; Mark 11:1–11; Luke 19:28–44; John 12:12–19).[9] On that occasion, the crowd greeted him shouting 'Hosanna! Blessed is he who comes in the name of the Lord' (Mark 11:9; Matthew 21:9; John 12:13). Hosanna is the Greek rendering of *hoshiah na* (Hebrew for 'save, please'), and the whole phrase is taken from Psalm 118:25–26. Its use in this context is hardly accidental, as parts of that psalm (esp. vv. 22–23) were thought to refer to the Messiah (cf. Matthew 21:42; Luke 20:17; Acts 4:11–12).[10]

However, whereas in Psalm 118 the words *hoshiah na* are addressed to Yahweh, the God of Israel, those who had gathered to greet Jesus now ask him, not his heavenly Father, to save them. He, they were hoping, was the one who had come in the name of the Lord[11] in order to intervene in the course of history and save them from Roman oppression. Matthew and Luke also tell us that, when Jesus later lamented over Jerusalem, he too explicitly identified with the figure in Psalm 118:26 (Matthew 23:39; Luke 19:38; cf. also Luke 13:35).

In order to grasp why the people understood the above quote from Psalm 118 in a liberationist sense, we need to take a brief look at the psalm itself. It in turn contains a few references that take us back even further in Israel's history, to one of the most important events in the life of God's people, i.e. the exodus from Egypt. This connection is most apparent in Psalm 118:14, which quotes from the song of deliverance sung by Moses and the Israelites after the crossing of the sea (cf. Exodus 15:2).[12] In the light of these allusions, the cry of Jesus' followers, 'hosanna – save us', gains in significance, because it illustrates what the people were hoping he, the Messiah, had come to accomplish. They were longing for another exodus, for Roman rule to come to a speedy end and for the kingdom of the Messiah to take its place.

Yet, as the story unfolded, it became clear that God's kingdom was not of the kind his people were expecting.

Neither was the Messiah. He even quoted all the wrong passages. While it was all right for him, and those telling his story, to make use of texts such as Psalms 2, 110 and 118 (which celebrate and proclaim the victory of God and his Anointed), no one would have dreamed to hear from the Messiah's lips the laments of the suffering and the persecuted. Yet, in addition to the royal victory songs, cries of anguish and despair (such as Psalms 22, 31 and 69) also have a crucial role to play in the New Testament accounts of Jesus' earthly ministry. Most astonishingly, the Gospel writers even combined these seemingly incompatible sets of texts in order to show that the victory of the Christ was won through the pain of his suffering.

When we looked at the Psalms as the prayers of the Christ, we noted that, in his darkest hour, Jesus aligned himself with Israel's downcast and downtrodden, using their language to give expression to his own sorrows – as well as to his trust in God. More than that, according to John 15:25 he even regarded what was happening to him as a fulfilment of these ancient texts.[13] The Gospel writers therefore took their lead from him when, in telling the story of his suffering, they time and again came back to the Psalms.

Mark, for instance, reports that the people offered Jesus 'wine mixed with myrrh' (Mark 15:23), and again that one man offered him a sponge with wine vinegar (v. 36; cf. also Matthew 27:34, 48; Luke 23:36; John 19:29). This brings to mind the sixty-ninth psalm, in which the psalmist complains that his enemies 'gave me vinegar for my thirst' (Psalm 69:21). At first glance, it might seem as if the offer of a drink was an act of kindness. But the psalm makes it clear that it

was a vile and brutal deed. Luke underlines this in connect-
ing the offering of vinegar with the soldiers' mocking of
Jesus (Luke 23:36).

In the passion narratives, we also have echoes of Psalm 22.
Thus, when the passers-by mock Jesus, shaking their heads
at him (Matthew 27:39; Mark 15:29), they do exactly what
the psalmist complains people were doing to him (cf. Psalm
22:7). Likewise, according to the Gospels, the chief priests,
the teachers of the law and the elders tease Jesus saying, 'He
trusts in God. Let God rescue him now if he wants him, for
he said, "I am the Son of God"' (Matthew 27:43). Israel's
religious leaders are here portrayed as siding with the
enemies of the psalmist, who too had been told that as 'he
trusts in the LORD; let the LORD rescue him' (Psalm 22:8).
This ironically puts the authorities on a par with the Roman
soldiers who, by dividing up Jesus' cloths and casting lots
over them, also act like the psalmist's adversaries (Matthew
27:35; Mark 15:24; Luke 23:34; John 19:24;[14] cf. Psalm
22:18).

McCann helpfully summarizes the overall thrust of Psalm
22, which moves from complaint and petition (vv. 1–21) to
exuberant praise (vv. 22–31).[15] Interestingly, the second part
of the psalm is not referred to in the Gospel accounts. Yet
those familiar with the Scriptures knew that neither the
psalmist's opening cry of abandonment (Psalm 22:1; cf.
Matthew 27:46; Mark 15:34) nor the enemies' mockery of
the one they thought had been abandoned by God (Psalm
22:8; cf. Matthew 27:43) were the final word. At the end, the
psalmist addresses his fellow believers affirming that God
'has not despised or disdained the suffering of the afflicted

one; he has not hidden his face from him but has listened to his cry for help' (Psalm 22:24). Indeed, the author of this remarkable psalm envisages that

> All the ends of the earth will remember and turn to the LORD,
> and all the families of the nations will bow down before him,
> for dominion belongs to the LORD
> and he rules over the nations.
>
> Posterity will serve him;
> future generations will be told about the LORD.
> They will proclaim his righteousness to a people yet unborn –
> for he has done it.
> (Psalm 22:27–28, 30–31)

The psalm thus witnesses to a God who does not forsake the afflicted – though in the deepest depths, this it what they, and their enemies, might be inclined to believe. The psalm also speaks of a God who comes out victorious, triumphing over his and the sufferer's foes, thus redeeming the one who put his trust in him. It comes as little surprise, then, that Psalm 22 played such a crucial role for those who had come to understand that Jesus' death on the cross was not the end of a failed would-be-Messiah but a turning point in the history of this world. It was the beginning of God establishing his rule over all the earth, just as the psalmist had envisaged many centuries ago.

REFLECTION

- Read Psalm 22 and reflect on the psalmist's suffering. How does the psalmist experience it, and how does he react to it?
- Does the use of Psalm 22 in the context of Jesus' suffering and death shed new light on the problem of suffering?
- The crowd who greeted Jesus on his entry into Jerusalem with quotes from Psalm 118 had quite specific expectations as to what the Messiah had come to do. Yet later on, with Jesus hanging on the cross and their hopes dashed, they all left him, presumably putting their hope in someone (or something) else.

  Reflect on your own ideas about Jesus, who he is and what he stands for.
- Turn your thoughts into prayer.

Reflecting on the Significance of the Christ: The Psalms in the Rest of the New Testament

Turning from the Gospels to the book of Acts, one finds that the first Christian sermon, Peter's Pentecostal speech, in which the apostle proclaims the resurrection of the Christ, again cites the Psalms (cf. esp. Acts 2:25–35). In addition to the quote from Psalm 16:8–11 already mentioned above, Peter also refers to two royal psalms, in which the focus is on the Davidic king. The first of these, Psalm 32:11, says that 'The LORD swore an oath to David, a sure oath that he will not revoke: "One of your own descendants I will place on your throne …"'. Peter applies these words to the Christ, the descendant of David, who at his resurrection has been placed on the royal throne. In fact, Peter implies that this is what the psalm is about because David, who was a prophet, saw 'what was ahead [and] spoke of the resurrection of the Christ' (Acts 2:30–31).

Following the lead of his master, Peter also made use of Psalm 110:1 (cf. Acts 2:34–35). But he wanted to make a different point. In the Gospels, the text is used to demonstrate that the Christ is more than being simply the son of David (he also is David's Lord; cf. Matthew 22:41–46; Mark 12:35–37; Luke 20:41–44).[16] Peter, on the other hand, focuses on the words 'sit at my right hand', which he understands to mean 'at my right hand *in heaven*'. And as David clearly did not ascend to heaven, the passage is taken as referring to the ascension of the crucified, who has been made 'both Lord and Christ' (Acts 2:36).

Again in line with the Gospel writers (cf. Matthew 21:42; Mark 12:10; Luke 20:17), Peter on another occasion mentions the saying about the rejected stone (Psalm 118:22), affirming that this too refers to Christ. He has become the cornerstone (Acts 4:11) so that salvation can be found nowhere else than in him (v. 12). Even before Pentecost, Peter is reported to have commented on the fate of Judas Iscariot, the disciple who betrayed Jesus, by combining two passages from the Psalms (Psalms 69:25 and 109:8; cf. Acts 1:20). The point of the speech in Acts 1:21–26 is that Judas' apostolic ministry had to be given to somebody else. This, according to Peter, is demanded in particular by Psalm 109:8, which expresses the wish that another may take the place of leadership that had belonged to the wicked.

The apostle Paul, in his proclamation of the gospel of Christ, also drew on the Psalms. In a manner similar to Peter, he quoted Psalms 2:7 and 16:10 (as well as Isaiah 55:3) to demonstrate that Jesus had been raised from the dead, and that he had not seen decay (Acts 13:32–37). The way in which Paul quotes Psalm 2:7 ('You are my Son; *today* I have become your Father') is interesting, because, in contrast to the Gospel writers, he does not drop the word 'today' (cf. Matthew 3:17; Mark 1:11; Luke 3:22 and also Matthew 17:5; Mark 9:7; Luke 9:35), which in Psalm 2 refers to the day of the king's coronation. This may suggest that, according to Paul, 'Christ was enthroned as Son of God by the resurrection from the dead'.[17]

But it is the letter to the Romans that, more than any other book in the New Testament, demonstrates Paul's indebtedness to the Psalms (as well as to the Old Testament in general). For instance, in Romans 3:10–18 we have a series of six quotations, all but one of which have been taken from the Psalms.[18] The passage is intended to prepare Paul's readers for his conclusion that the righteousness from God can only come 'through faith in Jesus Christ to all who believe' (Romans 3:22).

What is so interesting about the references to the Psalms is that Paul here quotes from the laments, which complain about the attitude and the behaviour of the wicked. In these psalms, the focus is on those who are indifferent about God and his rule, and who oppress and ridicule those who believe in him. According to Paul, however, all this talk about the fools and the wicked applies to everyone. Thus, the words of the poet, who struggles as he feels forlorn among all the evildoers, are *literally* true: 'there is no one righteous, not even one; there is no one who understands, no one who seeks God' (Romans 3:10–11; cf. Psalms 14:1–3; 53:1–3). Similarly, when Paul later in his letter talks about the hardening of those Israelites who have rejected the gospel, he quotes from a curse directed against the enemies of the psalmist: 'may their eyes be darkened so they cannot see' (Romans 11:9–10 cf. Psalm 69:22–23).

Paul's use of Psalm 44:22 in Romans 8:36, by contrast, illustrates that for the apostle Jesus had, in a way, taken the place of God (though this is, of course, *not* literally true). For while the psalmist was thinking of Yahweh, the God of Israel, when he said that 'for your sake we face death all day long', for Paul it is Christ for whose sake Christians may encounter difficulties and suffering. In line with the authors of the Gospels, Paul also makes Christ the speaker of Psalm

69:9 (cf. Romans 15:3). But whereas in the Gospels, it is the first part ('zeal of your house has consumed me') that is quoted, Paul focuses on Christ's experience that 'the insults of those who insult you fall on me'.

In his first letter to the Corinthians, Paul affirms the rule of the Christ saying that 'he must reign until he has put all his enemies under his feet' (1 Corinthians 15:25). Even death, the last enemy, will be destroyed because God 'has put *everything* under his [i.e. the Messiah's] feet' (v. 27). These words are taken from Psalms 110:1 and 8:6, and both passages are applied to Christ. The second one is particularly interesting because the psalm speaks about human beings in general, stressing that God has made them rulers over the works of his hands. But, of course, if this is true of humankind in general, then how much more does it apply to Jesus Christ, the true man. And as far as the promised defeat of death is concerned, Hans-Joachim Kraus has rightly stressed that this 'carries us deep into the Psalms, in which death is seen as a hostile power and its defeat is hoped for'.[19]

Another New Testament book that abounds with references to the Psalms is the letter to the Hebrews. The first two chapters contain a chain of nine quotations from the Psalter, which are used to demonstrate Christ's superiority over all imaginable powers and forces.[20] Again, this opening passage shows how the first Christians used the Psalms in order to explain and defend the notion of the Lordship of the one they had come to regard as the long-awaited Messiah. Thus, words that in their original setting in the Psalter refer to the king, humankind in general or God himself are now seen to find their ultimate meaning and fulfilment in the person and the work of Jesus Christ.

According to the author of Hebrews, not only is Christ superior to the angelic powers but his priesthood also far outstrips the Levitical one. This is demonstrated with reference to Psalm 110:4, where it is said of the king that 'You are a priest forever, in the order of Melchizedek' (cf. Hebrews 5:6; 7:17, 21).[21] In Hebrews these words are applied to Christ whose priesthood is a permanent and eternal one (cf. esp. Hebrews 5:9–10; 7:23–25).

Melchizedek is the priest–king, who in Genesis 14:18–20 appears quite out of the blue and vanishes as quickly as he had stepped onto the scene. The fact that he is not mentioned in any of the numerous genealogies in Genesis is taken by the writer of Hebrews to mean that he had no father or mother. Indeed, he was 'without beginning of days or end of life'. Thus, for Jesus to be a priest in the order of Melchizedek means that his priesthood is an everlasting one (Hebrews 7:3). More than that, Jesus is the true king of righteousness (this is what the name Melchizedek stands for) and the king of peace, just as Melchizedek was the king of Salem (Salem meaning 'peace'; cf. Hebrews 7:2).

It is also worth mentioning the quote of Psalm 40:6–8 in Hebrews 10:5–7. Again, the words of the psalmist are taken as the words of Christ who, being aware that God is not interested in sacrifices and offerings, proclaims that he has come to do God's will. The author of Hebrews here affirms that what was true of the psalmist of old, whose desire was to live according to the law and will of God, is true even more of Jesus Christ, God's own son.

Finally, to round off this section with an example from the last book of the New Testament, it is interesting to note that in Revelation the judgement and the rule of the Messiah are described in the words of Psalm 2:9. Thus, this royal psalm that proclaims the God-given dominance of the Davidic king over all the enemies of God and his people will eventually come true. The Messiah, the child of the woman (Revelation 12:1–6) and the rider of the white horse (Revelation 19:11–21), is after all going to rule the nations with an iron sceptre. He will accomplish what the kings of Israel never really managed to do (cf. Revelation 12:5; 19:15).

REFLECTION

- The sheer number of quotations as well as the ways in which the Psalms are quoted by the New Testament writers suggest that the early Christians seem to have been 'at home' in the Psalter.

  How do we think and feel about the Psalms? For instance, could we say that we are 'at home' in the Psalter?

- What can we learn from the ways in which the New Testament writers used the Psalms?

- Read Psalm 110 and picture Jesus as the one being described. Turn your thoughts into prayer and praise.

The Psalms and the Body of Christ, the Church

The numerous New Testament references to the Psalter are a telltale sign of the importance the Psalms had for early Christianity. This impression is confirmed by those passages that relate the psalms, in one way or another, to the Church as the body of Christ. To start with, there are some indications that some psalms were sung and prayed by the first Christians (cf. 1 Corinthians 14:26;[22] Ephesians 5:19; Colossians 3:16). To be sure, we do not know for certain whether these were the psalms found in the Old Testament – though this is by no means unlikely. However, the use of the term *psalmos* in itself, even if it referred to 'modern' psalms, underlines the continuity with the Jewish heritage. As Kraus put it, the first Christians, the Gentiles had now entered 'the world of Abraham and David, where the Psalms had been sung and prayed'.[23]

In the book of Acts we get a glimpse of the early church using the Psalms in their own prayers, trying to make sense of the bewildering things that were happening to them (Acts 4:24–30). Thus, in a remarkable example of contemporary application, King Herod, Pontius Pilate, the Gentiles and – most shockingly – even the people of Israel themselves are identified with the raging nations of Psalm 2. They are the enemies of God, they are people who plot in vain against the Lord's Anointed (Psalm 2:1–2), against his 'holy servant Jesus'.

The author of the letter to the Hebrews uses an extensive quote from Psalm 95:7–11 in order to admonish his readers to be obedient to God (cf. Hebrews 3:7–11). In fact, the entire section Hebrews 3:7–4:11 is built around this quote, to the extent that two of its parts are repeated twice. The threefold citation of Psalm 95:7–8, 'Today, if you hear his voice, do not harden your hearts …', in Hebrews 3:7–8, 15 and 4:7 underlines the urgency of the author's appeal not to persist in sin, lest his readers squander the chance to 'enter into God's rest'. That there is a real danger of it happening is driven home in the words of Psalm 95:11, 'So I declared on oath in my anger, "They shall never enter my rest" ', which are cited in Hebrews 3:11, 4:3, 5. The effect of these repeated quotations is that Hebrews 3:7–4:11 reads almost like a sermon on Psalm 95:7–11, in which the words of this old song are made relevant for the current situation of the book's recipients.

The book of Revelation, finally, depicts the singing of psalms as one of the hallmarks of the new age. It envisages the twenty-four elders and the 144,000 singing a new song (Revelation 5:9; 14:3). This is exactly what the psalmists had encouraged their congregations to do in response to the Lord's marvellous deeds (cf. Psalms 33:3; 96:1; 98:1). In Revelation 15:3–4 the faithful sing 'the song of Moses … and the song of the Lamb':

> Great and marvellous are your deeds,
> Lord God Almighty.
> Just and true are your ways,
> King of the Ages.
> Who will not fear you, O Lord,
> and bring glory to your name?
> For you alone are holy.
> All nations will come

> and worship before you,
> for your righteous acts have been revealed.

Some believe that this song is based on Psalms 86:9–10 and 145:17, although it does not follow those passages closely. Yet it certainly breathes the spirit of the Psalms in affirming the reign of the Lord. And it shares the vision of both, psalmists and prophets, that one day all nations will acknowledge the deeds of the Lord, and will worship the King of the Ages.

REFLECTION

- Paul, as we have seen, encouraged his readers to sing and pray the Psalms. Reflect on the different types of psalms found in the Psalter (i.e. laments, psalms of praise, thanksgiving psalms, etc.).
- How might singing and praying the Psalms enrich the spiritual life of our church and of ourselves?

FOR PRAYER

Lord, teach me to pray.
Lord, teach me to praise.
Lord, teach me gratitude, openness and honesty.
Lord, teach me to sing.
Lord, teach me to do all for Jesus' glory.
Amen.

3. Reclaiming Israel's Ancient Songs and Prayers

Much more could be said about the use of the Psalms in the New Testament. But it is hoped that this brief sketch has shown that the Psalms were alive and an important part of the life of the early church. It appears that Jesus and his followers knew them well and put them to regular use. They drew on them in their worship and prayer, in telling the story of the Christ, in reflecting on the significance of his message and ministry, and they applied the teaching of the Psalter to their own lives. In all this, the first Christians were reclaiming the Psalms for the present. They were making Israel's ancient songs and prayers their own, allowing them to transform their lives.

As we hope this book has shown, the Psalms have much to offer in terms of comfort and re-assurance, instruction and warning, but they also hold many challenges and are, at times, quite unsettling. Some may be more easily digestible than others, but it would seem that the early followers of Jesus did well in giving them the attention they deserve. So, to phrase it in Jesus' words, let's 'go and do likewise' (Luke 10:37).

Questions/Activities

1. How and in what way do the New Testament writers connect the Psalms with Jesus?
2. Why do both the royal victory psalms as well as those that talk of human suffering play such an important role in the New Testament?

3. Why were the Psalms in general of such great importance to Jesus and the apostles? Are they of similar importance to us, or should they be?
4. Apart from in connection with Jesus, how else are the Psalms used in the New Testament?
5. In the light of how the Psalms have been used by the first Christians, how can we apply them to our own lives?

Notes

1. J. Clinton McCann, Jr., *A Theological Introduction to the Book of Psalms: The Psalms as Torah* (Nashville: Abingdon, 1993), 163. Cf. also James L. Mays, *The Lord Reigns: A Theological Handbook to the Psalms* (Louisville, KY: Westminster John Knox, 1994), who regards the confession that the LORD reigns as the theological foundation of the Psalms.
2. See S.E. Gillingham, *The Poems and Psalms of the Hebrew Bible* (Oxford: Oxford University Press, 1994), 265–8, for this threefold approach to the Psalms.
3. Dietrich Bonhoeffer, *Psalms: The Prayer Book of the Bible* (Minneapolis: Augsburg, 1974), 19.
4. Ibid., 20–1.
5. See Gillingham, *Poems*, 266–7.
6. Ibid., 264.
7. Quoted from Geza Vermes, *The Complete Dead Sea Scrolls in English* (London: Penguin, 1998), 489.
8. McCann, *Introduction*, 163–75; see also William A. Holladay, *The Psalms through Three Thousand Years: Prayerbook of a Cloud of Witnesses* (Minneapolis: Fortress, 1993), 115–21.
9. Scholars are unsure as to why John includes the episode at the beginning of his Gospel while the other gospel writers

put it after Jesus' triumphant entry into Jerusalem (cf.
Matthew 21:12–16; Mark 11:15–18; Luke 19:45–48). The
best explanation seems to be that John uses the story in a
programmatic fashion, introducing his readers early on to
the significance of Jesus' death and resurrection (cf. John
2:18–22 and also the references to the 'Lamb of God' in John
1:29, 35, which appear to have a similar programmatic
function).

10. Hans-Joachim Kraus, *Theology of the Psalms* (tr. Keith Crim;
Minneapolis: Fortress, 1992), 193.

11. This too puts a new angle on Psalm 118, as in v. 26 'he who
comes in the name of the LORD' is the believer who comes
to the temple in order to worship God.

12. See McCann, *Introduction*, 167–8, for further details.

13. Even though in John 15:25 the words 'they hated me
without reason' are said to be written in the 'Law', they are
in fact a quotation from Psalms 35:19; 69:4.

14. John, by the way, explicitly informs us that this happened so
that the Scriptures might be fulfilled.

15. McCann, *Introduction*, 169–74. For a fuller treatment see
Ellen F. Davis, 'Exploding the Limits: Form and Function in
Psalm 22', *JSOT* 53 (1992), 93–105.

16. According to the Gospels, Jesus also quoted Psalm 110:1
in front of the Sanhedrin, affirming that he is the Christ,
and that his prosecutors would one day 'see the Son of
Man sitting at the right hand of the Mighty One and
coming on the clouds of heaven' (Mark 14:61–62; cf.
Matthew 26:63–64).

17. Kraus, *Theology*, 183.

18. For vv. 10–12 cf. Psalms 14:1–3; 53:1–3; v. 13a cf. Psalm 5:9b;
v. 13b cf. Psalm 140:3b; v. 14 cf. Psalm 10:7a and v. 18 cf.
Psalm 36:1b.

19. Kraus, *Theology*, 188.
20. The quotations are Hebrews 1:5 (Psalm 2:7); v. 6 (Psalm 97:7); v. 7 (Psalm 104:4); vv. 8–9 (Psalm 45:6–7); vv. 10–12 (Psalm 102:25–27); v. 13 (Psalm 110:1); 2:6–8 (Psalm 8: 4–6) and 2:12 (Psalm 22:22).
21. See also Hebrews 5:10; 6:20; 7:3, 11.
22. The NIV reads 'hymn' in this verse but the Greek text has *psalmos.*
23. Kraus, *Theology*, 179.

Reading List

Commentaries on the Psalms

Allen, Leslie C.
Psalms 101–150. (Word Bible Commentary 21; Waco: Word Books, 1983)
One of the three-volume WBC on the psalms. Each volume being written by a different author is both a pro and a con – the reader gets different perspectives on the psalms, but the whole is not so coherent. Breaking the volumes into sets of 50 may have eased the publishers job, but it does not reflect awareness of the importance of the canonical shape of the psalms! Allen focuses mainly on discussion of the structure of the psalms and their genres, and includes strong exegetical analysis.

Craigie, Peter C.
Psalms 1–50 (Word Bible Commentary 19; Waco: Word Books, 1983)
First of the three WBC commentaries. Craigie provides good exegetical insight into each of the individual psalms within his remit, and discussion of the New Testament approaches to these psalms. Helpful for preachers/bible

study leaders, if you are discussing individual psalms and their meanings.

Kidner, Derek
Psalms 1–72 (Tyndale Old Testament Commentary; Leicester: IVP, 1973)
Psalms 73–150 (Tyndale Old Testament Commentaries; Leicester: IVP, 1973)
Good exegetical analysis of the individual psalms. Comments are brief, dealing with the themes which each psalm brings up.

To be fair, all of the above commentaries were written before discussion of the canonical shape of the Psalter had really come to the fore.

Mays, James L.
Psalms (Interpretation Bible Commentary; Louisville: John Knox Press, 1994)
Mays has a strong approach to both exegesis of the individual psalms and the canonical shape of the whole Psalter. This is a very helpful, one-volume commentary.

McCann, J. Clinton
The Book of Psalms (New Interpreter's Bible Commentary; Nashville: Abingdon Press, 1996)
Along with Mays, McCann is one of the main proponents of a canonical approach to the Psalms, so not surprisingly McCann stresses the interpretation of individual psalms and the themes found in the book as a whole. Very accessible commentary, McCann seeks to apply the psalms to the realities of contemporary life, with lots of helpful illustrations.

Tate, Marvin E.
Psalms 51–100 (Word Bible Commentary, 20; Dallas: Word Books, 1990)
The third of the WBC volumes in order of writing, and deals with matters of canonical shape of the psalms as well as good analysis of the individual texts.

VanGemeren, Willem A.
Psalms (Expositor's Bible Commentary; Grand Rapids: Zondervan, 1991)
Again, there is strong analysis of the individual texts, without a great deal of discussion about how they relate to one another. There are brief comments on each psalm and good discussions of the christological implications of the psalms.

Other Helpful Books on the Psalms

Calvin, John
Heart Aflame: Daily Readings from Calvin on the Psalms (Philipsburg, NJ: P & R Publishing, 1999)
365 daily devotional readings from the psalms based on Calvin's commentary on the psalms. The title of this book explains its intent ... to set your heart aflame.

Lewis, C. S.
Reflections on the Psalms (London: Fontana, 1960)
This is a helpful discussion, particularly in relation to the difficult and troubling questions that arise out of the Psalter.

Longman III, Tremper
How to Read the Psalms (Leicester: IVP, 1988)
This is a good, basic introduction to Hebrew poetry and how to read and interpret the psalms.

Mays, James L.
The Lord Reigns (Louisville: Westminster/John Knox Press, 1994)
This excellent book is a collection of articles that Mays has written on the psalms over the years. Some of these articles have greatly influenced the way in which scholars undertake the study of the psalms. It contains strong analysis of the Psalter's theology with its central focus on the reign of God.

McCann, J. Clinton
A Theological Introduction to the Books of Psalms: The Psalms as Torah (Nashville: Abingdon Press, 1993)
In many ways this is another groundbreaking book. McCann reads the psalms as a book and discusses the significance of psalms as God's torah (instruction) for his people. Highly recommended!

Miller, Patrick D.
Interpreting the Psalms (Philadelphia: Fortress Press, 1986)
A good introduction to understanding the different genres of psalm – lament, hymn of praise etc. – with a helpful exposition of 10 psalms at the end of the book. Also includes helpful advice on how to read Hebrew poetry.

Peterson, Eugene
Working the Angles (Grand Rapids: Eerdmans, 1987)
This has an excellent chapter on the psalms and spirituality

from which we took the title for this book. For a fuller treatment of the psalms by Peterson see his *Answering God* (San Francisco: Harper and Row, 1989)

Zenger, Erich
A God of Vengeance?: Understanding the Psalms of Divine Wrath
(Louisville: Westminster/John Knox Press, 1996)
A helpful discussion of the imprecatory psalms, that is the angry ones which we do not really know how to deal with! Zenger helpfully discusses their role in the Book of Psalms and their place in the Christian church.

Glossary

Alphabetic acrostic psalms
These are psalms that employ each successive letter of the Hebrew alphabet at the start of each verse or series of verses (v. 1 begins with 'A', v. 2 with 'B' etc.).

Beatitude
A wisdom saying or proverb that indicates a lifestyle which will lead to God's blessing.

Canon/canonical
The canon is the final form of the biblical texts as we have them in our Bibles today. A canonical approach is one that takes seriously the shape of each book, so each passage is read and understood in the light of its place within that book. This is the approach we have adopted in this book in relation to the psalms.

Covenant
This is the relationship between God and his people which is firmly based on promise. There are various different expressions of covenant throughout the Old Testament (e.g. the covenant with Abraham or the covenant with Moses), but the essence of covenant relationship is that God

promises to be our God and we promise to be his people (Gen 17:7).

Genre

This term refers to the type of literature which is found in a given text. Contemporary examples would be journalism, poetry, novels etc. Examples in the Psalter would be lament, praise, royal and wisdom psalms. Each text should be interpreted in light of its genre.

Hermeneutics/hermeneutical

Hermeneutics is the process by which we read and interpret the scriptures and apply the lessons of each text in our contemporary context.

Lament

A type of psalm in which the Psalmist expresses a complaint to God resulting from the difficult situations faced in life.

Messiah

This comes from the Hebrew word for 'anointed one'. It was often used to refer to kings, priests and prophets in the Old Testament, and the New Testament authors apply it as a title to Jesus as the fulfilment of these offices.

Pentateuch

The first five books of the Old Testament – Genesis, Exodus, Leviticus, Numbers, Deuteronomy.

Psalter

Another name for the book of Psalms.

Torah
In its broadest understanding Torah can refer to all of God's revelation or instruction to humankind. Sometimes it is used exclusively to refer to the Pentateuch. In English translations of the Bible it is usually translated as 'law'.

Wisdom psalms
This is a particular type of psalm which reflects upon the 'big questions' of life and theology e.g. creation and the way of righteousness as opposed to the way of the wicked.

Yahweh/LORD/God
Yahweh is the name by which God chose to reveal himself through Moses to his people (Exod. 3). This is a proper name by which God presents himself as the covenant God. It is normally translated as 'LORD' in English versions of the Bible. The authors in this book use Yahweh, LORD, and God interchangeably in this volume.

Our Lenten Group at Oakridge